YOU NEVER TOLD ME THAT!

YOU NEVER TOLD ME THAT!

A CRASH COURSE IN PREPARING YOUR KIDS FOR INDEPENDENCE

KATHLEEN DAVIS

LIONCREST
PUBLISHING

YOU NEVER TOLD ME THAT!

A Crash Course in Preparing Your Kids for Independence

ISBN   978-1-61961-679-0 *Paperback*

978-1-61961-680-6 *Ebook*

CONTENTS

___

ACKNOWLEDGMENTS 9

INTRODUCTION 13

1. THEY'RE LEAVING, NOW WHAT?.................... 27

2. DON'T TAKE IT PERSONALLY 51

3. IT'S NOT (ALL) ABOUT YOU!......................... 63

4. TEACHING THE BASICS............................... 99

5. THE NEW HOME(WORK)................................137

6. WAIT—I HAVE TO TALK TO MY KID ABOUT WHAT?.............157

7. SOLVING THE BIG PROBLEMS 173

8. BETTER THAN OKAY 193

ABOUT THE AUTHOR 209

ACKNOWLEDGMENTS

———

I'd like to thank the many people without whom this book would not have been possible. The entire gang at Book In A Box publishing, Wow! What an incredible group of professionals. You have taken me from a person who was writing with the hopes of figuring out how to turn my thoughts into a book into an actual author. I will always be grateful. Special thanks to Tucker Max, who believed in my idea; Jeremy Brown, who held my hand the entire time and walked me through the process; Molly Gage, who helped me organize my ideas into an actual story, and Jeannette de Beauvoir, who worked tirelessly and patiently listening to my stories and helping me edit them. There were many more people involved, and to all of them I am thankful.

I want to thank all the people who graciously shared their stories with me and allowed me to take a few liberties to illustrate my points. There were so many people who shared their personal connections to these themes. To Adam Rupp and Anjali Luthra, who first gave me the idea to contact Tucker Max while I was at their home on a listing appointment. To Pam and Barry Trilla and Gina McNally, who I met at their bar, Barrique, in Lake Geneva, Wisconsin, for the role they played in helping me choose a title. To Susan Arts, who I met on an airplane on the way home from a convention in Las Vegas, for her thoughtful feedback. To Kay and Donkayote Arnold from Topeka, Kansas, who I had the good fortune of talking with at the pool at the MGM Grand Hotel, for their feedback, stories, and encouragement. To Jeff Wenzler, author of *The Pivotal Life* and producer of *10 Dollar Perspective*, thank you for your guidance and suggestions and for leading the way. To all of my amazing friends who supported me and assured me that the story I wanted to tell was one that people would want to hear. It would be impossible to name everyone, but I must mention Steve and Lisa Lyons, Laurie Graham, Eric Pilling, Margaret and Andy Slupecki, Beth and Mike Treptow, Karen and Jamie Newton, Jeanne and Mike Jaskolski, Mimi Singer and Jaddy Dupoy, Jean and Andy Dole, Russ and Claudia Johnson, Kate and Tony Marino, Pam and Paul Miller, Laura and Rob Oberheide, Yvonne and Ken Ostermann, Jim and Kim Wong, Craig and Valerie Becknell, Marla Brandt, Marsha Hammond, Robin Drumm Nuckols, Jenny Strom, Karen Morway, Kate Niedzielski, Julie Zielinski, Gina Whealan, Cindy Carlson, Dan Kass and Rachel Beyer, Scott Adams and Michelle Battle, Lisa Blue, Dennis Miller and Julie Schuppie, Julie Bulgrin, Eileen Nelson, Anne Davis, Rania Dempsey, Jen Hellmann, Amy Taylor and Jason Diamond, Tom Ellis, all the crazy, funny, wonderful girls at Mahjong (This is like a hidden Mahjong!), Christina Pruhs, Anne Mees, and to Jennifer Dragseth, who I look up to as a writer and person and who was inspirational in my decision to tackle this goal.

I am full of appreciation for Mark Davis who co-parents with me every day to raise children we are both so proud of.

An especially warm thank you to my mom and dad, who taught me to work hard, do my best, treat people well and find the funny in life where you can. Also, words cannot describe my thanks to Ted Perry, who always believes in me. I appreciate the support of my sister Elisabeth, brother-in-law Brian, niece Madeline and nephew Ryan, my brother Dan and sister-in-law Fran, and my grandmother Lorraine, who at ninety-eight years old is one of my favorite storytellers.

Finally, I want to thank George and Henry, who may have thought originally that this was a questionable idea but went along with it anyway, worked with me to find stories they could live with telling, and were relieved (I think) when they discovered that all the times they saw me on the sofa with my computer in my yoga pants that I wasn't just hanging out but was working on this book. You are the reason I want to be the best person I can be. You inspire me every day. Wherever life takes you, it will be exactly the right place, and I will be somewhere nearby cheering for you. I love you both!

INTRODUCTION

———

It's four o'clock in the morning. I'm wide awake, staring out at the darkness, and my heart is racing. The image that woke me? My son Henry falling off a cliff.

This isn't as far-fetched as it might seem. Henry is a climber, and any mother who imagines her son climbing is also going to imagine him falling. But this dream didn't just have to do with mountains; Henry was getting ready to graduate from high school and would soon be leaving home for the first time. It had suddenly occurred to me that there were a lot of symbolic mountains in the world for him to fall off of.

We know that one of a parent's most important jobs is to prepare children to leave the nest, and yet a lot of parents don't actually address it deliberately, head-on, or with concrete plans. In fact, I couldn't find *any* books that told me adequately how to prepare Henry and his younger brother George for going out on their own! This was in stark contrast to the dozens of books that over the years had told me how to toilet-train them, prepare them for the first day of school, and handle adolescent outbursts. The literature was strangely silent on the topic of leaving home.

Maybe there's a reason for that. Maybe a lot of parents are in denial about their children leaving. Maybe parents dread losing control. Maybe they don't trust their children to do the right thing. Or maybe they doubt their children's ability to make a life for themselves once they're out on their own.

Whatever the reasons, I knew one thing's for sure: I wasn't the only one who was lying wide awake and worrying at four in the morning.

* * *

Henry is seventeen years old and, it has to be said, fairly clueless about life. He is smart, don't get me wrong—smart bordering on brilliant. He's insanely bright about the things that he's interested in.

Henry climbing in Northern Wisconsin

For all his brains, it seems, at times, that he has little or no common sense.

Here's an example. Last summer he went to a leadership camp in Washington, D.C., and took a class on national security at American University, and he excelled at each, earning a perfect 4.0 and college credit for the class. While he was there, I flew out to see him, and we visited both American and Georgetown University.

We both fell in love with Georgetown. Now, the truth is that Georgetown's a reach for anyone—its acceptance rate is around 13 percent. But that fact actually provided great motivation for Henry because Georgetown has an amazing school for foreign affairs, and that's what he planned to study.

We went back home, and he started filling out his application. He was working on it one morning and had to stop because he was due at work. Off he went in the car, and soon thereafter I got a phone call. Henry was panicking. "Mom, you have to come here immediately!" he yelled.

I knew that Henry tends to overreact, so I told him to calm down and explain what was going on. He was at the self-serve gas pump. "This doesn't work," he told me. "The pump doesn't work, and I've already put my card in! You need to come here! It's not working!"

My brilliant son, who was applying to an extraordinarily competitive college, was in a panic because he couldn't figure out how to make a gas pump work. It didn't work the way he wanted it to work, the way he thought it should, and so he gave up, freaked out, and called me.

I talked him through it, of course. "Squeeze the handle slowly," I said, "if it clicks, you're going too fast." But all I could think was, *This is why you're calling me? What's going to happen when a real problem comes up?*

Yet another reason to be awake at four o'clock in the morning.

It's not just feeling impatience about how Henry handles situations like pumping gas, though. It's everything. Somehow, we seem to think that kids learn things by osmosis, by watching how we handle situations, by just using their common sense. We don't realize that much of this has to be taught.

Time management is an example of something we have to teach. The gas pump incident prompted more middle-of-the-night questions for me. *Will Henry be able to manage his time? Will he keep up with his college classes and the commitments he makes? Will he be able to plan?*

To be honest, I don't personally understand Henry's issues with time management and planning—I'm absolutely religious about keeping my calendar. Everything goes in it. If I ever lost my phone, I wouldn't know what I had to do next. But Henry never used the calendar function on his phone, and the planners that the school sent home with him stayed in his backpack. It was only recently that his father and I mandated he use *something* to keep track of his responsibilities and commitments. We ended up buying him a large-size day planner, and we've had to make sure he writes everything down in it.

I get that everyone's different, but there are some skills everybody needs to have. It will be interesting to see what happens next year when Henry's at college. We're not going to be there to make him keep a written calendar, so he's going to have to figure it out on his own. His father and I hope he'll do so without some disaster forcing his hand.

But here's the lesson we need to give kids getting ready to leave home: If you miss something now, the consequence isn't necessarily that dire, because you've got backup— your parents. But if you miss a class or a test in college, you don't get a chance to do it over again. Nobody's going to be as forgiving as your parents are.

And keeping a calendar is just a small part of it. There are so many things that seem completely obvious to adults that simply aren't a part of a kid's way of thinking. Kids are going to need to make a fast transition from having their parents to fall back on to being responsible for themselves. As parents, we need to be willing to help our kids prepare.

Part of that preparation is realizing how quickly situations can get serious. As adults, we imagine that kids will know how to behave in an emergency, but they don't. A few years ago, a high school student in our community died of an overdose. Her friends didn't know what to do, so they left her in a driveway—and that was where she died. That was another time that I popped out of bed, shaking, at four in the morning, imagining my kid in that situation.

The day I heard about the overdose, I took the direct approach and asked Henry what he would do if one of his friends overdosed.

"Aren't you supposed to drop them off at the front door of the hospital so you can get them help?" he asked.

I looked at him in horror and quickly realized that I was going to need to be very specific here. "If this happens, here's what you do," I said. "Even if you think you're going to get in trouble, you dial 911. You deal with the rest of it later." And it wasn't just about dealing with the emergency of an overdose. I was finally getting it: Everything had to be spelled out to him. "If you've been drinking, you call me," I told him. "If you can't get me, you call Uber. The questions can come later. You won't be in trouble. What *will* get you in trouble is *not* doing those things. The consequences will be far worse if you don't do them."

I imagine some parents think that if they talk to their kids about what to do in the case of an overdose or some equally terrible event, then they're tacitly giving the kids permission to do drugs, to be around overdoses. But the truth is that your child is going to make mistakes. Parents are kidding themselves if they think that their child isn't ever going to have a drink or go to a party. They can hope their kids aren't going to be out doing any drugs, much less heroin or ecstasy or anything else that's dangerous, but it's quite likely that they're going to find themselves in a situation in which *someone* is. What will they do? I don't like to think about Henry being anywhere near someone who is overdosing, but I would rather have him know what to do than not. Having a plan in place that you reiterate more than once—dial 911 if someone is in trouble, call Uber if you've been drinking—doesn't mean that a disaster will happen, but it *does* mean that your child will be prepared for it if it does. It's important to get them thinking about what could happen in advance so that they're not just reacting to what is going on around them.

These are situations that would be frightening for anyone, and no one is at their best in a frightening situation. But by talking about situations like these ahead of time, your child gets a chance to consider what their decision might be. If a situation does arise, then you can hope their instincts will kick in and they'll think, "Okay, I remember, we talked about this."

My nephew had a baseball scholarship at Wisconsin Lutheran College in Milwaukee, and midway through his freshman year, his roommate—also on a baseball scholarship—suddenly moved out of the dorm. At first, we had no idea why. It turned out that the roommate and his friend were driving around one night and decided it would be fun to catch some air coming up over a big hill. They did—and collided with another car, injuring an entire family. No one died, thankfully, but there were serious consequences. The roommate lost his scholarship, had to leave school, and even went to jail for a time. This kid was eighteen years old, and suddenly the rest of his life was affected by a split-second decision he'd made to do something he perceived as all fun and games. Now, instead of playing baseball in college, he was suddenly in jail. In just a moment, he'd gotten himself a mark on his life that will last forever. Knowing that small decisions can have a big effect is a lesson we can all use, but it's especially true for kids, who pretty much think they're invulnerable.

The point here is that parenting isn't *always* about allowing your kids to make mistakes on their own and learn from them. We have some responsibility to prepare our children for possible consequences of their actions as much as we reasonably can. What's obvious to us is most definitely not obvious to them! And preparing them (and ourselves) for independence isn't obvious, either.

BE YOURSELF

One of the ways you *can* prepare your kids for dealing with making mistakes is by being yourself and letting them see that. When your kids experience difficulties, let them see that nothing is easy or automatic for you, either. Let them see you stress out over a problem. If they think you're perfect, then they'll feel they can never live up to those standards. Showing them that life can throw you curveballs and letting them see how you confront those problems will help them understand that everyone deals with difficulties every day.

I've certainly had more than one opportunity to show my boys that navigating life situations isn't always easy. My life became a financial nightmare after my divorce. I hadn't asked for money when we separated. We each just walked away, and neither of us had a nest egg to fall back on. I assumed that I'd be able to make things work.

But then the stress of my situation distracted me so much that I couldn't work, couldn't produce results. I'm a realtor, and my income went from about $180,000 a year to $40,000 in one fell swoop. Suddenly, we had no money. We had to sell our house, which was a tremendous blow, because we were friends with everyone on the block and they'd been a tremendous emotional support for me and the boys. Thankfully, my sons and I eventually found ourselves a nice little place. My parents bought it, and I rented it from them. But that didn't solve everything.

I sold half of my personal possessions to try to make ends meet. I sold my bicycle, my camera. I just kept looking for things I could sell to get it all together, to make it through. I borrowed money from my parents. I remember thinking, *Well, I guess I could always be a stripper—oh, wait, I can't. My boobs aren't big enough!* When you're trying to support two children, you don't even know what you're doing sometimes. You grasp at straws; you imagine the unimaginable. It was an insane time. I would never want to go back to that moment. For about two years, it was a struggle, and that struggle took me to some pretty dark places.

At some point, I just made a command decision that I was done. That was it. I just couldn't be in that space anymore. I couldn't bear it for one minute longer. Several things happened that accelerated my decision. My dad was diagnosed with cancer, so I had to sell our new house, and then one of my friends committed suicide.

I saw it all as a sign that I had to make a change, so I just worked hard—incredibly hard—and then, suddenly, my business went crazy (in a good way). Within a year, I ended up being the number-one producer in the office. Thankfully, finally, my financial troubles went out the door, taking a good deal of my stress with them. We'd never gone on a family vacation, so I made it a priority that the kids and I go away every year. That year, I took them away on a fabulous vacation for the first time to celebrate.

Henry and George with our snorkeling guide in Tulum, Mexico

That started me thinking. What else could I do with the kids that I'd never been able to do when I was married? What did I want to show them while we were living together? I hated thinking that the only thing I was showing them was this weird upheaval in their lives, these stressful situations.

I wanted to make sure that they had a better picture of how to live, so I started being much more deliberate about how to make decisions and how to communicate.

Of course, that doesn't mean I always get it right. There have been a lot of times when I've wondered exactly what it is that I've been teaching them and times when I feel like I have it all wrong. But *that's* a teaching tool, too. Now, I remember to say I'm sorry when I get it wrong so they can see that I make mistakes and that I own those mistakes. There isn't just one right way to do everything—or, in fact, anything. We try things, and sometimes they work, and sometimes they don't, and we learn all this as we go along.

CHOICES HAVE CONSEQUENCES

Every decision carries a consequence with it. You hope that your kids will never make choices that will lead to bad outcomes, but my feeling is that, in general, you need to deal with things head-on. You need to talk about the issues, acknowledge that they exist.

Some things are difficult to talk about. As I said, you hope your kids will never have to make choices that lead to bad outcomes. But the only way they can make good choices is if you discuss those options with them—show them your take on an issue and encourage them to think it through rather than pretend it doesn't exist. I think that your kids will be a lot less likely to be in those situations if you talk about them. Your way of solving a problem might be different from theirs, or even mine, for that matter. But giving your kids a way to deal with a situation is better than not acknowledging it at all.

Identifying the myriad of choices, decisions, and problems ahead and talking about how to confront them is what's at the heart of this book. So, welcome to my world! We're going to look at ways that you can help your kid and yourself navigate this very tricky time—this time when they're getting ready to leave your home—and at the end of it, for everyone to be all right. No, at the end of it, I want everyone to be *better* than all right.

And maybe talking about what's to come for you and your child will keep *you* away from those lonely four o'clock mornings!

CHAPTER ONE

THEY'RE LEAVING, NOW WHAT?

So your kid is about to leave home. Are they ready to face the world on their own? Hardly! This time is filled with pressure for everyone involved. It can also feel like a referendum on parenting—how well you did, where you succeeded, where you failed. You feel vulnerable, and your kid feels vulnerable, too.

But there's still time to do something about it.

YOUR WORLD ISN'T THEIR WORLD

I think one of the reasons it's so difficult to prepare kids to go out on their own is that their experience will be so radically different from what our experience was. Not that ours was necessarily a piece of cake. I think about what it was like for me setting out for the first time, and I remember just how scary the whole thing was.

Of course, I *thought* I was totally prepared for college. I'd always been super-independent. I was the youngest of three kids, with a sister almost three years older and a brother just one grade ahead of me. Maybe because I was youngest, I was always the one bucking all the family traditions, the one who wanted to go far away to school, to get out of Wisconsin.

When I was sixteen, I had a job playing Bugs Bunny at Six Flags in Illinois. A lot of my coworkers were from Chicago, and I saw them as sophisticated, big-city, self-assured. I always thought I was like them. I took risks. I always aimed high; there was pretty much nothing I didn't think I could do. I think that I probably didn't know what it was I was supposed to be afraid of.

I decided to go to school far away, in Georgia, to the Savannah College of Art and Design. It was 1987. My parents and I loaded up two cars to move me. I had an old Volkswagen Jetta and somehow managed to get all my stuff into it and my parents' car. I even had a jar sitting on the front seat next to me with my fish Wooby in it. I thought I had it all together. I was positive I knew *everything*.

My dad has always been inventive; he's an engineer and will think things through. This was in the pre-cell phone era, so he hooked us up with CB radios so we could stay connected, my parents in their car and I in mine. I wanted to lead the way, of course—I'm pretty bullheaded—even though I had no idea where I was going. But we set out with my car in the lead, and every ten minutes or so, my father would call me on the CB and tell me something, for example, that I was driving too fast, which, of course, annoyed me no end.

Somewhere in Tennessee, the CB suddenly started crackling. It was my father's voice. "You missed the turn! You missed the turn!"

So here's the thing: The problem with CB radios is that reception isn't always 100-percent and, naturally, it failed at this precise and unfortunate moment. I was lost. I had pulled off at one exit, they had pulled off at another. I had no idea what to do. Should I just sit there? Should I go somewhere else and maybe get reception? The questions were endless. This went on for hours.

Literally.

Somehow, we finally found each other, and I'd more than learned my lesson. Needless to say, *I* followed *them* after that. I'd wanted to run the show and exert my independence. But I wasn't even close to being ready to. The truth is that I was terrified, and I'm sure that they were, too. As a parent myself now, I can imagine how they must have felt.

Cell phones and GPS devices aside, there are a lot of challenges facing kids applying to college today that I didn't need to worry about.

Just start with the college application process itself. I applied to one college, I got in, and I went there. Pretty linear. I've talked with other parents who are my age or even ten years younger, and that was their experience as well. They applied to one college, maybe up to three—but not ten or fifteen or even twenty, which is what some kids are doing today. These days, five colleges represent a bare minimum. The average is eight. It's stressful, exacting, and expensive to put in all these applications.

I made sure that Henry looked up all the information about all the colleges, and together, we created a spreadsheet.

Henry's Colleges

School	Acceptance Rate	Size	Graduation after 4yrs / after 6yrs / first yr ret.	Total Cost	Percentage of New Students Receiving Aid	Average Amount of Aid (Grants)	Average Amount of Aid (Loans)	City	Majors	Average ACT	SAT Req or other	Average GPA	Application status	Deadlines	Decisions	Henry's rankings for colleges with acceptances
American University	29%	13,061 (7,706 undergrads)	76% / 82% / 88%	$60,586.00	71% grants 65% loans	$22,854.00	$6,840.00	Washington DC	School of International Service BA	Comp 28	common app ACT plus writing - 2 letters (teacher/counselor) Mid-year report -	3.7	Turned in 11/11/16	Early dec. Nov. 10 Early dec. 2 Jan 10 Reg. Jan 10		
St. Edward's University				$58,000.00	90+ %	$18-26,000	unknown	Austin, TX	Global Studies / Political Science	Comp 25	common app ACT plus writing - 2 letters (teacher/counselor) Mid-year report -	3.5	Turned in rolling admission	May 1 is absolute deadline		
Oregon State	78%	30,592 (24,612) undergrads	32.3% / ? / 84.8%	$45,100.00	67% some help	unknown	$11,453 of some sort	Corvallis, OR	International Relations / Political Science	Comp 25	common app. ACT, essays, letters	3.5	Did not apply	Feb 1		
Lewis & Clark	63%	(2209) undergrads	66.2% / 72%/ 83%	$61,536.00	90% some help	unknown	$41,863 of some sort	Portland, OR	International Relations	Comp 29	common app.ACT essays, letters	3.9	Turned in 12/28/16	Jan 15		
Seton Hall	76%	9,627 (5,817 undergrads)	56% / 66% / 85%	$51,780.00	97% grants 59% loans	$21,829.00	$10,422.00	South Orange, NJ	School of Diplomacy & International Relations	Comp 25	common app or Seton Hall app	3.5	Turned in 12/2/16	Feb 1		
George Washington University	38.5%	25,613 (10,740 undergrads)	76% / 83% / 93%	$65,260.00	77% grants 42% loans	$25,770.00	$7,994.00	Washington DC	International Relations	Comp 29	common app- test scores optional	3.5	Turned in 12/28/16	January		
College of William and Mary	33%	8,437 (6,299 undergrads)	83% / 90%/ 95%	$55,330.00	35% grants 26% loans	$16,386.00	$6,842.00	Williamsburg, VA	International Relations - with St Andrews	Comp 31	interview at the school is important - common app - subject tests	3.79	Turned in 12/28/16	Jan 1		
University of Denver	73%	(5,758) undergrads	66.6%/ ? / 86%	$62,277.00	70%	unknown	$36,190 of some sort	Denver, CO	International	Comp 28	ZeeMee, common app	3.71	Turned in 12/28/16	Jan 15		
Hawaii Pacific University		(3663) undergrads		$39,336.00		unknown		Honolulu, HI	International Studies, Bachelor of Science and Diplomacy and Military Studies	Comp 22	common app	3.34	Turned in 12/28/16	Jan 15		

College spreadsheet

And then there's the cost of school tuition, which is—to say the least—prohibitive. State schools cost between $25,000 and $26,000 a year. The cheapest private schools are $45,000 or $50,000 a year; many are $60,000 to $65,000. I wouldn't have even dreamed of those numbers when I was a kid.

(Of course, I wasn't exactly paying attention to the numbers back then. It would never have occurred to me that someone had to pay for my college, that someone might have to stress out about finances, or that someone was doing the worrying for me. I never thought of that because I never thought about anyone but myself. It's a normal, natural thing for children and adolescents, but it's one more problem to add into the mix.)

THE COMPETITION IS TOUGH

Beyond concerns about tuition and fees, our kids face an extraordinarily competitive atmosphere as they get ready for college. A 4.0 GPA average would have landed you in most colleges back when I was growing up. Now? Not so much. Henry goes to an extremely challenging high school. If you have anything below a 3.5 GPA, then you're in the lower percentile of the high school. There are a lot of kids with amazing GPAs, so you can just imagine the pressure on kids like my son.

I would have been wearing a dunce cap at his school.

These days, a 4.0 GPA isn't what it used to be, especially when you're trying to get into college. That's the minimum requirement, and it has to be supplemented with many other things—participation in activities, volunteer work and internships, and spectacular projects. There are a lot of other things that need to be done for someone to get noticed, set apart, and seen as great college material.

You have to think about all of those factors—and think about them while your child is still in high school—because while going to school and engaging in activities, your child is in effect creating a résumé for college admission. The numbers are staggering. I think our high school has about eighty-five clubs that kids can join—or they can start another club, a new club, and show their creativity that way. It's hard for a kid to be confronted with so many choices. How do you even begin to choose? What criteria do you use? How do you stand out? It's enormous pressure. At what point do kids feel like they're good enough?

There's pressure on them to be creative, inventive, and prescient about their outside activities as well. And here's what's difficult for parents: kids have to take hold of those activities on their own. You can't be the one planning your child's visit to Hunger Taskforce to package up food for the poor, because colleges will be onto you. You can't suggest that your kids do the volunteer work you wished you'd done at their age or connect with the nonprofit agency that you like. Our kids need to be the individuals that *they* want to be, and then they have to go out into the world and go after what *they* want. Many colleges these days will only allow kids to list a few extracurriculars; they want to see passion about something rather than a quantity of activities. No one is going to respect kids if they just do what their parents want them to do. They'll be found out pretty quickly, and so will you.

AND THEN THERE'S FACEBOOK

Transparency is another issue that we didn't have to face. There used to be a joke about something going on your "permanent record," but the truth is that we had nothing even close to the permanent record that kids have now. I made a lot of mistakes in college, but people forgot, no record was kept, and I could recover from them. Most kids just don't have that option these days.

Why? I have two words for you: social media.

When Henry was a freshman in high school, there was an incident in our community when some kids created an Instagram handle using other kids' names. They put up a page but made it look as though the other kids had done it. Later, it was traced back to some students who wanted to get the others in trouble by posting controversial and inappropriate content. It was meant as a joke—albeit a bad one—but it had terrible consequences.

The situation spiraled out of control very quickly. The school got involved. Parents got involved. The boys who posted the photos had to change the false Instagram handles, and the school wrote letters that stayed in the files of the kids who had been the prank's victims so that the erroneous information didn't follow *them* around.

Can you imagine putting that page up as a joke? Or any page that isn't squeaky-clean? Schools look at social media sites. Employers look at them. Everyone is going to see what's there. It could have been devastating for the victims' futures. I think about the boys targeted, both sweet kids on their way off to good colleges, and all the opportunities that could have been taken away from them if people had believed that they'd put those images up.

> *"Don't say anything online that you wouldn't want plastered on a billboard with your face on it."*
> —ERIN BURY

And that's what happened when the kids in question hadn't actually *done* anything. When kids *do* put questionable material on social media networks, they're jeopardizing not only their present, but their future. This is another example of kids believing that they're invulnerable, that bad things can't happen to them. Everyone acknowledges that the privacy ship has sailed, but most kids don't understand just how far over the horizon it's gotten.

Think about photographs, for example. Especially questionable photographs. They're everywhere. Snapchat was *designed* for the sharing of inappropriate content, for heaven's sake, with photos that disappear in three to ten seconds. (And you *know* that the first thing that kids do when they get a Snapchat photo is take a screenshot of that picture...so much for the content disappearing!)

This is one of those times when parents invariably respond, "Yes, but *my* kid would never do that." To which I say, "Um, no, your kid would *totally* do that." Because kids do it. (For that matter, adults do it, too. There are plenty of pictures around of adults who shouldn't have recorded what they've put online.)

We'd never see arrests for this sort of thing on the ten o'clock news if nobody's kids were doing it. Adolescent boys do send pictures of their penises to girls, and they do share photos of their girlfriends' breasts with their friends.

They don't do it because they want to be a criminal or even to be mean. They do it because they don't think about consequences or about how other people will interpret what they're doing. They do it because their girlfriend has hot breasts, and they just want to show them off to a friend. Then the friend's mom sees the picture on the kid's phone and calls the police, and suddenly people are talking about child pornography, and *that's* on the kid's permanent record, ready to follow them for their whole life. It spirals out of control in a *nanosecond*.

Even though my boys are smart, I know that learning about online behavior isn't a matter of intelligence. So I tell them the same things over and over.

Don't ever send anyone a picture of your penis. Don't do it. If you're stupid enough to do it, don't include your face. Don't ever do that. Don't be an idiot. You might go to jail. If some girl ever sends you a picture of her without clothing on, erase it right away. Don't keep it, and don't show it to anyone, and don't even think of forwarding it. It's pornography. You can't send naked pictures of people to others. Don't do it, especially when you—and the subject of the photograph—are under eighteen. In fact, don't do it at all.

Of course, whenever I say anything like that, they roll their eyes. "Oh, my God, Mom, do you think I'm an idiot?" *No, I don't, but someone in the world is an idiot, and I just don't want it to be you.* I'd rather have them roll their eyes at me and think I'm a total weirdo for talking about these things in such a frank manner than not saying anything and getting a phone call from the police.

I do think that these decisions around transparency are difficult for kids to make. They're putting themselves out on social media to be popular and fit in, and we all know that current relationships and social status are much more important to high school kids than what might—or might not—happen in the future. The future is a question mark. The present is immediate, real, and potentially painful.

There's a fine line, though, between warning kids of dangers lurking ahead and actually making the decisions for them, the decisions that they need to be learning to make. It's so much easier for parents to make those decisions. We know what's healthy and helpful and reasoned, and they don't. So as you're preparing your kid to leave, you have to be constantly monitoring yourself as well, making sure that you're not stepping over that line. In general, I think you'll know when you do, or your child will let you know. They might not do it verbally, but they'll let you know.

WHOSE CHOICE?

It's often difficult to stand back and let your kid decide. On anything! Choosing a college is an easy example. I could always tell when it was I who was suggesting a school versus when it was Henry making the choice. If he was persuasive, I would back off. I'm learning to ask, "Why do you want that? Tell me why you want to go there." It's got to be his choice, but having the conversation means that I get to see if he's thought his choice through. Does he like the school's awesome academic programs, or does he like the awesome climbing activities at the school?

It's worth checking out whether something is your kid's thought or yours. There are a lot of decisions that we *think* our kids are making when, in reality, our perceptions are actually about us. They're about our expectations of our kids. For example, Henry ran cross-country for three years. He *hated* cross-country. One summer, he ran almost ten miles a day—five miles in the morning and five at night—a ridiculous amount of running. But after all that training, he only completed one race the entire season. He just stopped in the middle of all the other races. He loved the camaraderie of the team, but not the races themselves. It finally dawned on his father and me to ask him if he liked what he was doing, whether he wanted to continue with cross-country. And he didn't.

Henry running cross-country

We thought we were teaching him the right thing by keeping him in cross-country. We thought we were teaching him not to quit, to stick to what he was doing. But when we figured out that it wasn't Henry who had chosen running, everything changed. We backed off from pushing him toward cross-country. He chose to do climbing instead, and his whole world changed overnight—his disposition, his enthusiasm, and his self-esteem. He went from being not confident at all and unhappy to being extremely self-confident. His grades improved. His posture changed. He became a different person, both because he enjoyed climbing and also because he was finally the one making the choice about how to spend his time.

I think that if you watch your kids, they'll tell you whether or not you're pushing your agenda on them. I also think that in your heart, you truly *do* know when you're encouraging your child to go in one direction or another. One way to find out is to ask yourself the question, *Would my kid be doing this if I weren't pushing so hard?* I think you know when it's you who's making the decision. Give your child options—to some extent, you can still control which options you present—and then say, "This is your decision. Here are some ideas." Your child is smart enough to make choices about many things. If they're having problems choosing, it may be because you're not giving them all the information that they need to make the choice.

Making their own choices is a major step in leaving the nest, and it can feel threatening because it shows that your child is moving toward a time when they won't need you anymore or, at any rate, will need you differently. That's scary! As parents, we spend most of our time thinking about how to keep our kids happy, how to keep them going to the next level, how to make sure they get good grades, that they have friends, that they succeed. Most of us think about ourselves, too, of course—how to keep ourselves happy, how to make enough money, how to advance our careers—but most of the time, we worry about our kids.

But then, seemingly out of the blue, comes the realization: *They're going to leave.* They're going to go off and live their lives somewhere else, and where does that leave us? Some of us realize this with a kind of panic—what do I do now without them to define me?—and some of us realize with dawning pleasure that now we can do things we couldn't do before. Either way, though, the thought changes our world, and the truth is that we end up finding *ourselves* in transition along with our kids.

PREPARE YOURSELF

I started thinking about all this earlier than some people because I was on my own. I think I was lucky, actually, because I was able to start thinking about this transition early on as an opportunity to change my career, maybe even move someplace else. My mind was exploding with ideas about what I could do to reinvent myself, my life. And looking at it from that positive point of view was very empowering. I often visualized a life of writing books and doing art, and when I started talking about it, the kids began to see me laying the groundwork for my future.

Instead of waiting until they leave, my suggestion is for you to do something *now* that you can roll into when they're gone. I think that's important for you. It means that it will be something you really want. But I also think it's good for your kids to see that you do have a life separate from them, and that that life is going to go on when they're gone.

Of course, our children will be a part of our lives in the future, and vice versa, and it's healthy to acknowledge this and show them that things will feel different as we spread *our* wings a little, too. Each of us, parent and child, want the other to be a part of whatever the future holds, but we're also acknowledging that things will be different.

I still am interested in what my kids are doing, of course. But I think that we all need to realize that it cuts kids a little slack when they realize they're not responsible for their parents' complete happiness. *And* it's going to protect you a little from freaking out completely when they walk out the door.

If you don't think about your kids leaving until they're packing up their things, then there's no real transition, and their departure is too much of a shock to your system. It's like jumping into a cold pool. Don't let that happen. Instead, think about what *you* might want to do in the next few years. When you look at it that way, the possibilities become endless, and you see the future filled with exciting options stretching out in front of you.

So find something to get excited about. If you haven't been working outside the home, are you going to go back to work when they're gone? Do you want to teach yoga? Do you want to take up a drawing class? Whatever it is you want to do, don't wait until the kids go. Start doing it now. Give your kids a special gift: the capacity and ability to start thinking about you more as a person and less as a role. That transition can start happening earlier if you let it.

DON'T LOOK NOW, BUT THEY'RE WATCHING YOU!

If you do start thinking about your future, your kids will learn a lot from seeing you take care of yourself that way. In fact, they're already learning a lot from you anyway, from seeing how you deal with all sorts of situations. Real lessons don't happen only when you sit down and have conversations about putting naked photos online; real lessons happen every day, too. Your children have been observing you all their lives, seeing how you treat people, solve problems, and deal with unwanted telephone calls. They may have walked through the room and heard you saying something, part of which stuck, even though they weren't trying to hear it.

When I think back to my childhood, I think about all the times I watched the way my parents behaved toward other people, interacted with them, and solved problems. Those are the lessons I learned best. I joke a lot about my dad, of course, but I also know that if my dad were having a rummage sale and selling a book priced at one dollar, and somebody offered him that one dollar, he'd probably say, "How about 50 cents instead?" That's my father's way of looking at people, and that's what I learned from him. He never had to tell me what to do or how to do it. He just lived his life, and I observed how he lived it.

He was always a giver. He loved making people happy. He did the same thing in his business. He taught me over and over while I was growing up that you work to do a good job, that you work to get the work done. The money comes later. You don't want to work only for the money. Money is a byproduct of working, of doing a good job. Work hard, he taught me, and then the rest will follow. Those were passive lessons that I learned from watching him, from living with him. He didn't always say the words out loud. He didn't have to. I just saw it every day.

I try so hard to show my kids the same thing. If you go out and rake someone's lawn and they don't pay you, it's okay. That will come back to you at some point. You should just treat people nicely. I hope those lessons have sunken in. I think that they have. Everyone's going to teach different lessons and have different values, but it's important to keep your actions consistent with what you want your kids to be learning. Just remember that you've said a lot of things *not* on purpose that far overshadow anything you have said on purpose.

Here's another example: I try not to swear. I grew up in a family where we weren't allowed to even say the word "God" unless we were making some sort of biblical reference. "Crap" was a swear word for sure; we would never have said that. We spoke very respectfully to our elders.

Then I went out into the world, and, of course, I observed that people swear, sometimes quite a lot. I picked up on it and, perhaps inevitably, I now swear occasionally. I tell the kids not to, and then swears come out of my mouth. My kids are smart. They say, "Okay, you can't tell us not to talk like that, and then *you* do. That's not acceptable." Of course, I come back with every parent's time-honored response. "First of all, I *can* tell you that, because I'm your mother!" But I know that they have a point, so I add, "But I understand your issue with it."

As I said before, kids watch everything you do, they listen to everything you say, and they remember. Especially, perhaps, the things you don't want them to remember.

If you do something you don't want them to do, you're going to have a hard time teaching your children not to do it, especially as they're looking to you to teach them how to be once they leave home. Still, doing something you don't want them doing can provide the opportunity for a lesson. So, for example, I might say, "If you swear, I personally think it makes you sound less intelligent, because there are smarter words you could use in that situation."

I'm a firm believer in knowing your audience and acting appropriately around that audience, so I'm very clear with my boys that what works in one context doesn't work in another. "I'm your mom," I say. "If you want to say disgusting things, don't say them in front of me. Go off with your friends in the basement and say whatever you want. Don't say it in front of me. I don't need to know what you're saying. I mean it. Why did you think that was okay to say to me? Don't do it!"

Again, I'm not always perfect—I'm actually *never* perfect—and I certainly don't always present the right example through my behavior. But even when I don't present the right example, I try to use it as a time to teach. "Okay," I might say, "I'm sorry. I shouldn't have used that word. You're right. I shouldn't have. Here's another option."

HELPING KIDS THINK OUTSIDE THE BOX

Of course, there are lessons that you *do* teach on purpose. For example, I'm a born salesperson, and when we moved out of our last house and into the one we live in now, we decided to sell some things. I wanted to include the kids in the process, so I asked them, "What's the best way to get the most money for things we want to sell? We have some nice things. If we put them on the front lawn and have a rummage sale, what'll happen?"

Henry said, "Well, people come over, and then they're like, can I have that for a dollar?" I was pleased he had figured that out. He understood the natural tendency to ask for a deal, and he also understood that if you value things properly, other people will as well. It's all in the presentation. So we worked together to create an estate sale rather than just a yard sale. I roped off our living room and dining room, I gave George a clipboard, and I put Henry behind a little antique table inside our house. We advertised, and we opened our house up for just one day, for only three hours, for this estate sale.

George stayed out front and allowed only nine people in at a time, just as they do at regular estate sales, and customers had to sign in on the clipboard. George signed people in, and Henry checked them out after they'd been through. I placed regular prices—good prices, in fact—on our things. I also told the boys to not be afraid to say "no" to any offers.

The boys were completely jacked about the sale. What they learned from this experience is that there's more than one way to do things. This sale could have gone one way or another, and they made the choice to value what they were doing, the choice to present things in a certain way. I've never believed that there's only one way to do anything. I've always felt that if you believe you can do something, you can do it. That was the lesson here. What boys want to sit with their mom at a sale in their house on a Saturday? But my boys had a ball. They had a great time doing it, and we had a very successful sale. I think they felt proud of what they were doing.

So sometimes the lessons work. But that doesn't mean that you're in for smooth sailing ahead...

CHAPTER TWO

DON'T TAKE IT PERSONALLY

———

No one likes transitions. They're difficult to navigate, especially when you don't yet know much about what you're transitioning *to*. Transitions are an uncomfortable time of not being *here* anymore and also not yet being *there*.

Transitions are a big deal for any of us. They're especially a big deal for kids. And many—if not most—kids show stress by acting out. A parent's job here is extraordinarily difficult and can be summed up in four words: It's not about you.

Remember, you already have some experience in not taking your kids' behavior personally. When your four-year-old threw tantrums, you reminded yourself that she was just testing boundaries and wasn't actually trying to ruin your afternoon. When your eight-year-old announced that he hated you, you remembered that he was feeling scared and didn't actually wish that you would die. So gird yourself up and tell yourself that this time, too, isn't about you, and chances are good that both you and your kid will survive this moment, just as you survived those other interactions.

It's easy, though, to look at your kid's behavior and see it as a reflection on your parenting. Or, in fact, a reflection on you, period. I read a book recently that gave readers four rules for living, and one of them was, "Don't take it personally." The more I think about this rule, the more I try to apply it every single day because I think it's a tremendous truth and the best advice in the world. We always look at everything in life as it relates to us, whereas the reality is that most people aren't thinking about us at all. That's the thing that's hardest to banish from our minds. We think, *They're looking at my kid. They're judging us. How does all this reflect on me?*

So the first thing to remember as your son or daughter starts the process of selecting a college to attend, for example, is that it's not about you. Kids' choices of schools are fraught with opportunities for parents to feel insecure.

We all want the best possible college experience for our children, of course, but there's still another voice lurking in the backs of our minds—the voice that says, *What will other people think about this school? Does my father expect my son to go to his school? Will people think I didn't encourage my child enough? Will they think that I drove my child too hard?*

FOCUS ON GETTING THEM READY TO LEAVE

The thing that you need to keep reminding yourself of is this: This transition is about your child and their future. I think that if you can pull back on your own emotions, you can let go of that nagging voice and all the insecurities that come with it. Otherwise, you're putting yourself in a situation that you just can't win.

If you're thinking about yourself, you're also taking something away from your children, I believe, especially in this time of transition, when your kids are starting to become adults. It's about *them*. I had to ask myself what it was that Henry wanted, and then I had to sit back and listen to him tell me. That wasn't easy! I had (and continue to have) some pretty strong ideas about what would be best for Henry, and I've never been shy about sharing those ideas. To shut my mouth and listen to Henry's ideas was extraordinarily challenging. I had to sit on my hands sometimes, and close my mouth, but the truth is that pretty cool things happened when I stopped talking, because Henry came up with ideas I would never have thought of. That's when his personality came out, and his journey began—a completely different journey from the one I would have sent him on. It's his. This is his time.

On the flip side, your kids are going to do some seriously messed-up things. Guaranteed. And when that happens, the temptation is for you to step in and stop it. So your kid will make some mistakes, and you just need to see how they play out.

The exception, of course, is when their behavior becomes dangerous. If they're doing something that will harm them or get them arrested, then that's where you step in and put a stop to it. Understanding that your child is behaving badly because they're scared of this transition is all well and good, but you don't want them to actually get hurt.

But other than that? I think you owe it to them to let them do things that aren't necessarily things that *you* would do.

COPING WITH YOUR KID'S FEARS

When your kid acts out, it's tough. I didn't realize how tough it was until last Thanksgiving break. Henry spent ten days having a good time, doing some climbing, and sleeping late. The night before school started back, though, he was suddenly having a meltdown. It turned out that he had about twelve hours' worth of homework for his AP government class.

I stared at him, aghast. "But you had the whole break to do it in!"

"It was a break!" he protested. "That means you don't work!"

"No," I said, the magnitude of the problem beginning to dawn on me. "It means you have more time in which to do it. It doesn't mean you don't do *anything*."

He just looked blank.

I tried again. "The whole rest of the free world understands, Henry, that during a break, you get time to yourself, but you also get more time to do your work, like a major project. You can't just do whatever you want the whole time and think you're released of your obligations to do anything!"

We argued for another hour, until it was ten o'clock. Then he started the homework—a tremendous amount of homework—and every forty-five minutes or so, he had a complete flip-out about it, screaming things like, "I am never going to finish this [expletive deleted] homework!" Then he just wanted to go to bed. And so did I.

I also had to look at his brother's reaction to all of this drama. George doesn't like conflict. He especially doesn't like chaos at home. So while Henry was doing his flipping-out routine, George was pacing around the house and muttering about school being difficult, even though he's a great student. "School is so hard, Mom. It's so stressful!"

Of course, I knew what was going on. George was extremely upset that Henry was so distressed. I told George to go to bed and try to sleep. I told Henry that he had to stay up until he was finished. Generally, I'm not quite that intense a micromanager, but I was seeing red. Henry had had the whole break to do this homework.

I started falling asleep around two o'clock that morning. George was still awake. He'd crept into my room at some point, an indicator of his stress level. This was a fifteen-and-a-half-year-old boy who generally didn't even want to be in the same *room* as his mother, much less sleep in her bed. Henry, meanwhile, stayed up and soldiered on through.

When I woke up, it was six o'clock, our usual time to get up for school. There was an index card taped to the wall in the hallway outside my bedroom where I'd be sure to see it. "Mom, I was up until 2:30 in the morning. I do not feel comfortable going to school this morning." I still have a photo of that note because I think it is so hilarious. *I just don't feel comfortable going to school this morning.*

He doesn't feel "comfortable"?

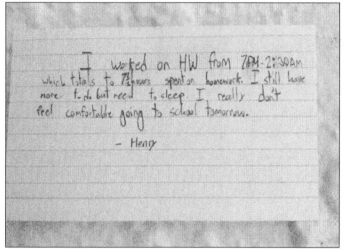

Note taped to the wall outside my bedroom door

Oh, really, I thought, *you don't?* I woke Henry up and told him to get back to his homework. I called the school and told them we had a family situation—I thought that described what was happening pretty succinctly—and that Henry would be in late. He finished his homework. He handed it in. He got an A on the subsequent test. It was a huge turnaround and a tremendous wake-up call for him. "I don't ever want that to happen again," Henry told me. *Good,* I thought.

Acting out can be painful for everyone involved; there's no question about that. And I think that it's tied to the issue of choice and having to make choices. Henry decided to apply to eight colleges, and in the beginning of the application process, I had concerns about how he would pick the schools. There's such a fine line between it being your kid's choice or yours. The stress involved of selecting schools can be debilitating.

I remember being with Henry at Georgetown. I loved that school so much that *I* wanted to enroll! I think that if they'd have had me, I'd have gone in a heartbeat. I was pretty sure that Henry would apply to Georgetown (though, in the end, he didn't). I think that he suddenly got terrified by the whole process and everything that lurked behind it—leaving home, being on his own, managing college, everything. His father and I had him on track for applying to West Point, and of course to Georgetown, and while we thought these were Henry's choices, what we actually saw was Henry trying to please us by following the direction he thought we wanted him to go in. And he couldn't keep it up, that pressure of doing what *we* wanted, along with all the other pressures.

So he lost it. He stopped handing in his homework for two weeks. I don't even think he could control it. He just shut down and stopped everything.

It was disastrous, of course. He was a senior in high school, and that behavior came close to shutting down any likelihood of his being accepted at *any* college. And it was so out of character. The phone calls started rolling in. What's happened to Henry? What's wrong? Why is he doing this? His AP government teacher sent his father and me messages. And we didn't know what was the matter, not at first.

But when I stepped back from the panic, I saw that our expectations were only exacerbating what was already a stressful time for him. Finally, we said, "Hey, you know what? You don't have to go to Georgetown." After missing two weeks of assignments, Georgetown was most definitely off the table in any case, and that was part of the message. "This has got to be your choice, but the things you're doing right now are going to dictate whether you get any choices or not. The fact that you didn't hand in any of your homework means that now you have fewer choices. We're going to step back. You can make the choices, but you need to know that you're making some pretty significant ones by not handing in any of your work. Let's just start over, and then you can decide what you want, because it's not about us."

You have to know how to pick your battles. There are times when it's best to let your kid deal with the consequences of their decisions and actions, and then there are times when you have to show a confused kid how life actually works. I think it's hard to know when you're right and when you're wrong, but I think it's just that you have to ask yourself, "Who needs to learn this? Is this my lesson? Is this his lesson?" It's not personal.

I didn't care if Henry's teachers thought I wasn't making him do his homework. What I cared about was that Henry wasn't going to know how to get his homework done when he left for college. All I wanted was for Henry to be equipped with the right skills when that happened.

But Henry's teachers were calling me, trying to find out what was wrong, and I'd be lying if I said that I didn't feel some pressure from them—pressure to give them a clear answer, even to absolve myself. When something like that happens, it contributes to the difficulty parents have with letting go of the sense that, on some level, it's about them. No parent wants their child to fail—not just for the child's sake, but also because *they* don't want to be perceived as a failure as parents. It's about the parent growing up along with the child.

I just want my child to be able to walk out the door and succeed. If that means failing now, then, ironically enough, I've succeeded.

The point of all this is that this last year of living together with your child is often one of the hardest you'll experience. Your kid is scared. No matter what they say, no matter how much bravado they show, the truth is that they're scared. And when people are frightened, they don't always behave well. Add in the still-developing adolescent brain, and you've got a great recipe for acting-out behavior.

So be prepared to navigate this transition knowing that your kid isn't always going to be at their most loveable. That's okay—you probably won't be, either!

CHAPTER THREE

IT'S NOT (ALL) ABOUT YOU!

You would think that, as parents, we already know that it's not about us. Once our kids arrived, suddenly our world was all about keeping them safe and well, about taking care of them. But then you come to this time when they're beginning to let go, and you're beginning to let go, and abruptly you start realizing that you want to keep on making their decisions for them. You suddenly want your kids to do what *you* think is best for them.

In the last chapter, I talked about how this is a time when a lot of kids act out. So there's something going on that you might think of as a kind of dance. Sometimes you're leading the dance, and sometimes your kid is, because it's a situation in which you're both trying to find your way.

One of the things that can help here is for you to be very clear and explicit around your expectations for their behavior. And then, once you've done this, brace yourself. It's a little like going to your doctor's office for a shot; sometimes, the anticipation is worse than the event itself.

And sometimes the shot really hurts.

KEEP YOUR SENSE OF PERSPECTIVE

Because of the anticipation and/or the actual pain, we parents are very likely to miss, or misunderstand, what's actually going on. Your kid is going to act out, period. It's not because of you or your parenting. It's about them and their need to distance themselves from you. Hear me: *They have a need to distance themselves from you.* Understanding that dynamic keeps you sane—sort of—and also helps keep things in perspective. A lot is going to be happening, and not all of it is catastrophic. Your kids may act crazy, and *you* may act crazy (or you might overreact, or they might overreact), but nothing that happens will define your entire relationship, nor will it define them as a person or you as a person. Events are generally neutral. We're the ones who put value judgments on them.

I think it's easy for parents to experience any of this acting out and then overreact to it instead of what's behind it, and that makes the behavior seem bigger than it is. So preparation will help. If you can tell yourself, *These things are going to happen, and when they happen I'll remind myself that it's just a moment,* it will be a lot easier for you. That's the mantra to use. *It's just a moment. A day from now, this moment will be over. I may even have forgotten it by then. So for now, I'm just going to get through it.* Keeping that perspective on what's happening will help. It has certainly helped me.

Hopefully, as your kids have been growing up, you've been consistent with them. You've been letting them know what is and what is not acceptable behavior. But it's easy to get into a heated argument with your kid. Sometimes, you're in the middle of one before you even know it's happening. This is why, sometimes, a healthy interaction means just walking away from a situation for a minute or more.

I'm pretty specific with my kids about my expectations of them. If something is happening that I think is completely unacceptable or out of control, they're usually aware of it, because by now we know what we expect of each other. I want to be spoken to in a courteous way, and in return, I don't speak to them discourteously. If I do, I apologize to them later. "I'm sorry I spoke to you that way," I say.

"I was upset and I shouldn't have. Next time, I'm going to try and do it differently instead."

The truth is that they're learning from you all the time. If *you* don't do what you want *them* to do, then they're not going to do it. It really is that simple. So pay attention to what they're learning from you, because they're going to take whatever it is that they learn from you with them out the door. Be clear on this: They're watching you all the time, observing the way you interact with your spouse or your friends, or the way you speak on the phone, even the way you talk to a customer service representative. The phone is a big one: I am constantly amazed by the number of people who have conversations on the phone that they should never, ever have in front of their kids. If you treat others disrespectfully, that's the way your kids are going to treat people. I'm big on showing what I expect.

MAKE EXPECTATIONS CLEAR

One day not too long ago, I was working across town from where we live, and I got a phone call from George, who was extremely upset with me because he and Henry had come home for lunch and found the door to the garage locked. We live three blocks from the school, so they come home to eat lunch and walk the dog every day.

Both boys were freaking out. "Where are you? Come home now! I can't believe you did this! We're not going to get to eat lunch! We're not going to get to walk the dog. Why would you do this? You're ruining our whole day! We can't eat lunch!"

As it turned out, I wasn't the person who'd locked the door, but that wasn't relevant. What was relevant was that I was in the middle of a business situation, trying to restrain myself and still speak to them nicely. I couldn't get a word in edgewise. I kept saying, "Listen. I am twenty minutes away on a work appointment. I'm just not going to be able to get there by the time you have to go back to school. I'm really sorry, but I can't do anything about it."

George just got more and more angry. Because of my tone, and because I wasn't jumping in the car and doing what he wanted me to do, he thought I didn't care. He kept calling me back, over and over, raising his voice more each time, and I kept saying, "George, I'm going to hang up now, because you're not getting the message, and I can't do anything about it."

Later, we sat down and talked about what had happened. I don't know that anything necessarily got resolved, since we each continued to see the situation completely differently. My point of view was that both boys have keys to the house, and it's their responsibility to carry those keys with them. Their point of view was that the door should have been unlocked for them, as it usually was. George was saying, "You never locked the door before," and he was right about that. I don't lock the door, so they didn't expect to find it locked, and that's why they didn't have their keys.

It's an example of where my expectations and the boys' expectations didn't coincide. My expectation was that they speak to me with respect. I didn't appreciate being screamed at while I was at work (or ever, for that matter). Additionally, I expected them to take some responsibility for dealing with the problem.

The boys' expectation was that I would come and save them, and they were shocked and angry when I didn't. To tell the truth, though, I wasn't all that sorry to see them in a situation where they could learn something. Life isn't always going to be perfect, kid, so deal with reality, not with what you want reality to be. The house is locked? Go buy a bagel.

BE CLEAR ABOUT CONSEQUENCES

As I said in the preceding chapter, there's going to be a lot of this acting-out behavior as kids begin to break away from home and think about being on their own. They want independence, but not the responsibility that comes with it.

Which brings us to punishment. Punishment is tricky.

For a long time, I felt like I was the worst punisher in the world. The truth is that I never wanted to punish my kids. Who does? You want your kids to like you, right? And, besides, sometimes the punishment hurts you more than it hurts them. Saying that they have to stay home on Friday night when you wanted to go out and are now stuck keeping an eye on them may be worse for you than it is for your kids.

So I've always subscribed to the policy of not giving my kids a punishment that punishes me more than it punishes them. Seriously: if the punishment makes you suffer more than it does the kids, then you may want to rethink it! It's okay to make mistakes, to change the punishment when it's not working, substitute it with one that makes sense instead.

You can avoid changes, though, by having a plan in place for punishments. Don't ever come up with a punishment while you're angry. If you do, you'll probably end up with something that sounds a little like, "And you're also never going to *ever* leave the house again, and you can't drive until you're fifty!" That's clearly not going to work, and besides, you'll probably regret the words the minute they leave your mouth. When you're angry or upset, you can't think straight, and you can't come up with good punishments.

So planning is key. Tell your kids upfront what consequences they'll face if they do something forbidden. If I say to my son ahead of time, "Listen, Henry, if I get your report card, and it says you haven't handed in your homework for a week and a half, you won't be able to use the car for a week." That makes sense. He knows about the punishment from the start, so he won't be surprised if it happens. This also enables him to make a better choice. Is the prohibited activity worth the consequence that goes along with it? He may decide that it is, but most often, he will decide that it isn't.

If Henry chooses to not hand in his homework, I can just say, "Hey, I saw your report card, and you didn't hand in your homework, so as you know, you're not going to be able to use the car." The consequence is rational. It makes sense.

The best thing about indicating consequences for breaking rules ahead of time is that it's excellent preparation for your kids' new lives—the lives they'll live once they move out of your home. Out there in the world, most activities or behaviors entail consequences that people know about ahead of time. If you don't show up for work for a week, you will be fired. If you rob a bank, you will be sent to jail. Most of the time, it's pretty clear what's going to happen as a consequence of decisions that people make, so why should your house be any different? Kids like boundaries. They like knowing what's what. What they don't like is irrationality—when rules change arbitrarily, or consequences aren't always the same. In those cases, they're unable to make choices because they're flying blind.

I've always been a person who likes lists, so I write down the rules of the house. Everyone can see them. Everyone knows what they are and what the consequences for breaking them are, too. What that shows my kids is that I care enough about them to teach them how to live in the world.

DON'T ENGAGE IN A BATTLE OF WILLS

If our kids learn one thing from living with us, it's that we parents make mistakes, too. I'm always trying to tell my boys that they shouldn't swear. Then something totally unexpected comes up, and suddenly I'm swearing like a drunken sailor. When that's happened, I've gotten hold of myself right away and said, "Okay, I shouldn't have said that." The reality is that, again, it's good for your kids to understand that you're a person. But you'd better be prepared to explain yourself and fess up. Then you can expect the same thing of them.

This is a decent lesson in itself. Sometimes, even the calmest parent is going to swear, but acknowledging it and apologizing for it goes a long way in terms of modeling good behavior. Encourage your kids to take responsibility for their actions by taking responsibility for your own. Say, "I'm sorry. I didn't mean to say that."

I think that, as parents, you're going to screw up; you're human. I know that *I'm* going to screw up at least ten times a day! But if I tell myself that I'm getting at least ten good learning opportunities in the process, then I'm putting things into perspective. You'll see opportunities like that, too. Seize them as much as you can.

YOU'RE STILL THE PARENT

Even though it's not about you, you're still the parent. So you need to be both prepared and reflective. And in some ways it *is* about you—it's about your reactions to the behaviors your kids are throwing at you. This is a good time to remind yourself that they love you. They're being jerks because they need to get their feelings and their fears out, and their parent is their safe space. I've had to remind myself of this more times than I can count. You need to react to what's actually happening beneath the surface, not to what you're seeing and hearing.

What you're seeing and hearing can in fact be very painful. Sometimes, I listen to my boys, and I think, *Oh my God, these people don't even like me.* We seem to be playing on completely different teams, an analogy I don't even like because it becomes about scoring points against each other, and that wasn't what I thought parenting would be like when my kids were born. It isn't what I signed on for.

And, of course, you can't have one uniform response because every child is different, and different things work with different kids. George provides me with a great example. He is extremely tenacious. He believes passionately in what he's saying, which I totally admire. He doesn't let go of things. He is like a pit bull sometimes. He might not like that reference, but when he feels that he's right, he's like a dog grabbing on to a piece of meat and won't let go.

What often happens is that, in response to George, I start playing the same game. I start doing the same thing, and suddenly we're both tugging and tugging against each other. And if I have any space at all in my head for reflection, I realize how ugly and truly mentally and physically exhausting it is to play that game. A lot of times I end up saying, "George, you need to go in the other room," or I decide that I should go into the other room. It doesn't matter who leaves. We just need to distance ourselves from each other and the battle that seems to be going on between us, because what is happening isn't healthy.

What happens 99.9 percent of the time is that George comes back to me. It's a sign of maturity. He comes back and wants to fix it. He says, "Mom, here's the reason I got upset," or, "Here's what I was thinking." Of course, if he didn't come talk to me once he cooled down, I'd be the one to reach out. But as a parent, I feel that it's important for me to encourage him to take that first step. Once he starts talking to me in a reasonable way, I'll start talking to him, and then we always work it out. It's that walking away for a minute that gets us both back on a better page.

Some people would say, "Don't walk away from somebody. Work it out." But sometimes walking away from the situation and breaking that cycle *is* working it out. It depends on the child. With George, that's an excellent tool. It reminds him that I'm a person who deserves better treatment, just as he does.

This is also a reminder for me that George does love me. I'm human. I need those reminders as much as anybody else. Sometimes, the whole thing can feel overwhelming, it can feel that at this stage of the game parenting is just one big struggle, and we're all prone to a little pity party from time to time.

Then, just when you least expect it, your child will come through with something wonderful. It may be the smallest thing, the most discrete indication of interest, perhaps a question such as, "What are you doing, Mom?" that's enough to make you feel better. Your kid comes just one step toward you, and this reminds you that they actually *do* want to be part of your life.

There's an invisible circle around each one of us, and sometimes when you have an adversarial situation with your kids, you feel like they've stepped outside your circle, and it's lonely in there without them. But then they do something that lets you know they want back in. As long as they take one step into your circle every once in a while, what they're saying, in essence, is, "See, look, I'm here. I'm in the circle with you." Then they'll go back out...until the next time.

The point is that they truly do want to be there with you. They're going to go as far away as they can—as far away as they dare!—but then they'll come back every time. As a parent, that doesn't always feel great. You probably feel like they're spending all their time trying to get out of your circle. But what they're trying to do is show you and themselves that they can be outside your circle and still be safe.

Ironically enough, that's exactly what we're trying for. Even though it's scary for both our kids and ourselves, stepping in and out of our circles is exactly what we want for them. It's a true dilemma. We want them to not need us, but then when they don't need us, we're terrified.

I was thinking about this recently, and it occurred to me that what I'm actually saying to my boys in my head is, *I want you to just let me know that if you needed somebody, it would be me.* That's what it is, I guess. I just want them to be okay, but if they're not okay, I want to know that either their father or I would be the one they'd turn to.

IT'S NOT SUPPOSED TO BE THE PARENTS' SHOW

You probably think that you know all this already. You know that it's not all about you. You've given your child constant love and attention for over a decade and a half. Isn't that enough proof that you know it's not all about you?

Well, not necessarily. I think that if you look around and observe parents interacting with their teenagers, it often does seem like it's the parents' show. I look around sometimes and find myself asking whether it was my kids or me making the decisions. I may be speaking from limited experience—from within the socioeconomic niche in which I live—but I know that a lot of parents consider themselves failures if their kids don't do certain things. If they don't try out for a sport, for example, or go to a certain summer camp, or get a tutor for the SATs. The problem with this is that the kids aren't given a wide enough net in which to capture their own dreams and desires.

On the other hand, I'm constantly impressed by parents who can say, "Eh, I don't know if he has lunch today," or, "I don't know what class she has, I don't know what she signed up for." I know that makes it sound like the parents don't care, but in a way, I think it's pretty cool.

When I encounter parents like these, I'm in awe of them, because I think that they're putting a lot of trust in their child. It makes me wonder what amazing things a kid accustomed to that level of trust could accomplish. I do try to follow their example in my own way. Whenever I get the opportunity, I try to step back and just let Henry or George figure out whatever it is on their own. Well, I *try*. It's not always easy. I think I micromanage a lot, but I'm not necessarily micromanaging the right things.

Remember when I talked about Henry and Georgetown? At the end of the day, Henry never really wanted to go to Georgetown. I think he thought the school was pretty cool, but I know that there were other things going on for him as well.

In fact, at one time—and maybe even still today—Henry wanted to be a dirt bagger. A dirt bagger is a climber who lives in a car, van, or even a tent and goes from mountain to mountain. To my mind, what we're talking about is a homeless person who's into climbing.

Henry loves watching documentaries about the pioneers of climbing, and I watched a lot of them with him so I could understand the things that he loves. A lot of these people lived in their vans, ate cat food, smoked pot, and just lived for the moment at the base of various mountains. A lot of the time, they were running from law enforcement because they weren't supposed to be living in the national parks. They were total rebels, but they were worshipped by a lot of people. Certainly, girls loved them. These climbers were risk-takers, constantly trying to scale mountainsides, and half the time, they were high when they did it. Getting high isn't Henry's thing, but he still thinks that these people are cool.

Henry likes the idea of risk-taking, which is funny to me, because Henry's never been a huge risk-taker. But perhaps his obsession with climbing is teaching him to take more of them. "Mom," he said to me, "maybe I just want to spend a year climbing. I kind of want to be a dirt bagger." I wasn't exactly thrilled, to tell the truth, and I responded out of that feeling. "What?" I said. "Wait a second. You're telling me that you just went through one of the best schools in the country in order to be a homeless person? That's the goal? Oh, my God. Are you joking?" I didn't even know whether to laugh or cry. I just didn't.

I don't know if Henry will ever be a dirt bagger, but he might. He was serious when he was talking about it. And if he does, I need to come to terms with it. I have to let go enough to let him make the decision, because it isn't about me. Part of me thinks that it's different, it's actually kind of cool, and the other part of me is screaming, *This is insane! People die doing that!*

The point is, I don't know what will happen, and Henry doesn't know what will happen, but it's his life, not mine. Maybe he'll like it and want to do it forever. Maybe he'll do it and then go off to a great college. But I have to silence the voice inside me that sees the following dialogue developing:

"What's your son doing?"

"Going to Harvard. What about yours?"

"He's a homeless person in a car at the foot of a mountain."

I often wonder this: If we asked our kids what it is they truly want to do, would we be able to predict their answers? Or would our answers reflect what *we* want them to do, what *we* want for them? If we're being honest, I think that it's the latter.

But not making our kids' decisions for them doesn't mean that we cannot at the same time be making decisions for ourselves, beginning to pursue what we want in life. It's healthy for our kids to see that we have a life apart from just being a parent, and that we're still growing and changing, too.

LET THEM SEE YOU DEVELOPING

A few years ago, I hired a business coach. I was pretty successful in my business as a realtor but was never very intentional about what I did. She encouraged me to plan out a strategy—not just for my business, but also for my life.

We talked a lot about how important it is to work to live rather than live to work, and she helped me set goals in that direction. Now every year, I have a forty-page plan

THE DIRTBAG DICTIONARY

DIRTBAG CLIMBER: a person who dedicates her or his entire existence to the pursuit of climbing, making ends meet using creative means. A dirtbag will get her food out of a dumpster, get his clothes from a thrift store, and live in a tent or vehicle to save money. Often found living near major climbing destinations, the dirtbag is a rebel with a cause who finds happiness in nature. When the dirtbag grows up (if ever), he or she often is drawn to a profession engaged with the outdoors and/or creative arts. —dirtbagging, dirtbagger, dirtbagged

BALLER DIRTBAG: This person is a dirtbag at heart, but no longer sacrifices all creature comforts of society, rather indulging in many of them. This dirtbag sports clean, brand-name clothes, and has the latest, most modern climbing gear. A baller dirtbag is defined by balling in one area of his life (i.e. gear, vehicle) and dirtbagging in another (i.e. food, shelter). An expert at finding a good deal in stores or online and then bragging about it for the next ten years.

BORN AGAIN DIRTBAG: The dirtbag that got tired of dirtbagging, entered the 9-to-5 world, and then returned to the dirtbag life. A renowned storyteller, this person will describe the horrors of spreadsheets, meetings, and awkward talk around the water cooler. Often lives in a van (see vanbag).

CLASSBAG: the dirtbag with class. This person has a flexible job (i.e. graphic designer, writer, photographer, etc.) in which she or he has to be professional and sometimes presentable. They have the skills to attract money for their services, and can follow through with the goods. Their friends know them as a dirtbag, and their employers know them as pros. Experts at time management and cleaning up for meetings just after climbing.

CLEAN DIRTBAG: a dirtbag with an obsession to stay as clean as possible. Always has hand sanitizer and baby wipes available within reach, and is constantly preoccupied with the conundrum of being a neat freak who loves living in the outdoors. A go-to source when you are out of toilet paper or forget something related to cleanliness.

CRUSTY DIRTBAG: an older dirtbag, usually male, who dirtbagged it for too long and is bitter about it. Often self-righteous, this guy misses the good old days and constantly reminds anyone who is listening why things were better when he was young. When no one is there to listen, he takes to online forums with his message, where he is more likely to find company. Also known as a glory days dirtbag.

DESK MONKEY DIRTBAG: the climber with a desk job who longs to live the dirtbag life but never has for extended periods of time. This person has a strong sense of adventure and a stronger sense for practicality.

that includes goals for both my personal and business lives, and I include at least one goal that has to do with other people. This year, one of my goals was just to think about other people more than myself, because it's incredibly easy to just set goals for improving our own lives without ever thinking about anyone else.

Here's what drove that goal. I went through a period in which I was frequently turning down invitations to do things with one friend or another. Sometimes, someone would text me and ask me to do something, and I might not even respond. I would intend to in my mind, and I'd think, *Oh, yes, I have to get back to that person,* and then I just wouldn't. None of this behavior was personal. I simply didn't make my interactions with others a priority.

This year, I literally wrote it down. "Think about other people more." And I'm not just talking about having nice, random thoughts. I was clear. "Think hard about how what you do affects other people," I wrote. "Think of positive things to do for other people." That was in my plan.

I'll admit that part of the reason for this goal was the recognition that my kids are still in my house for a couple of years—Henry just a half a year, and George two and a half years—and I want them to see me doing things for other people.

Cannot live without a house, health insurance, or reliable vehicle. The desk monkey dirtbag often begins their dirtbag existence with early retirement.

DIRTSTER: a rarely seen combination of half dirtbag, half hipster. While it is difficult to climb with an ironic personality and tight pants, these folks get it done. If questioned, the dirtster will deny their identity to protect their unique and sometimes endangered breed.

FAMILY DIRTBAG: dirtbags with children. This dirtbag is responsible at raising a family but also manages to save time for climbing. Their tent often has more square acreage than a college dorm room, but they are still well-versed in the dirtbag life. Kids raised by these types of parents either go on to become top climbers, abandon the lifestyle completely, or find a middle ground, like their parents did.

FANCY DIRTBAG: a female counterpart of the baller dirtbag, this woman can rough it but often does so with perfectly painted fingernails. Can crank out pitches with the best of dirtbags but also knows what kind of wine pairs best with dinner. Often has an addiction to websites like Pinterest and Etsy.

FRATERNITY DIRTBAG: guys who generally live in communal groups, commonly found in the towns nearest to major climbing areas. Although many possess college degrees, they refuse to grow up and get real jobs. Instead, they prolong their collegiate experiences with dormitory-esque lifestyles featuring ramen noodles, PBJs, and PBR. They still do laundry at their mom's house if she lives nearby. A fraternity dirtbag will abandon his living status as soon as he meets a badass climbing chick, but his buddies will let him have his room back each time if things don't work out.

POSER DIRTBAG: someone who wants to live the dirtbag lifestyle, does not for various reasons, and yet still looks similar to one. This person dresses similar to the dirtbag baller, has a subscription to outdoor magazines, and talks about making climbing trips but rarely does. A powerful force in the outdoor economy, this person rarely actually goes outdoors.

WORKBAG: a dirtbag with a full-time job. Found all over the country in towns and cities with climbing nearby. Often works "four-tens" (four, ten hour work days) and then heads straight to a big wall or crag for a three-day weekend. Also called a weekend dirtbag or a neo-dirtbag.

VANBAG: a dirtbag who lives out of their comfortable vehicle, most commonly a pimped-out van. Such a van may have a refrigerator, stove, solar panels and other plush accommodations. Easily ignites jealousy amongst dirtbags with lesser vehicles, especially on rainy weather days. Male vanbags use the line, "Do you want to check out my van?" to lure the opposite sex into their mating quarters.

—TAKEN FROM ERICA LINEBERRY, *THE CLIMBING ZINE*, VOLUME 5, THE DIRTBAG ISSUE

IT STARTS WITH US: EMPATHY

When we start talking about doing things for other people, it goes deeper than just carrying someone's groceries for them or visiting a friend in the hospital. One of the most important gifts we can give our kids before they leave home is the gift of empathy.

A lot of people feel that a person is either empathetic or they're not—that empathic behavior can't can be taught. I disagree. I do think that we have opportunities to teach empathetic behavior. And we have to start with how kids learn by example by watching their parents. The way you behave right there in your house is going to be observed, and your kids are going to carry that out of the home with them when they leave.

I've been getting incapacitating headaches since I was a little girl. My children have never known anything other than a mother who gets terrible headaches. Now, I'm on a medication that keeps them at bay for the most part, so I only get one or two a month. But when the kids were babies, I'd get headaches ten to fifteen times a month, headaches that were bad enough for me to leave work. It was a significant handicap.

Even when they were very young, my kids adapted to the situation. When they'd come home from school and see

I was in bed, they knew how to behave. The lights had to be off. They had to bring hot towels into my room and put them on my head. Almost from the start, even back when their father and I were still married, the kids knew how to make their own dinner. They learned how to put something together, because sometimes they were alone. Their dad was a professional musician who sometimes worked at night. They would be home with a mom who had a headache and a dad who was out playing a gig. They knew that they couldn't make noise, and that they had to take care of themselves.

Of course, I was there, and if I'd had to, I could have gotten out of bed and taken care of any situation that might have arisen. But in the meantime, my kids were learning empathy. They had to figure it out. They had to imagine how I was feeling. And of course, it wasn't always smooth. Their attitudes have gone from one extreme to the other. Sometimes they'd say things like, "I don't care, we're sick of your headaches, you always have a headache," but at other times, they said, "Here's a blanket. Let me turn up the thermostat. I love you, Mom."

There are a lot of different ways kids can learn empathy. Sometimes, we're quick to judge other people when they do things we don't like. I'm always asking the boys, "Well, why do you think that person did that?" or, "How do you think they feel?" It's important to be constantly pointing out places where they can develop empathy.

I've always asked those questions. I look at terrible situations—people who hurt others, who swindle, who lie, whatever the behavior is—and imagine the motive behind it all. *Why did they do that? What could make a person do that? They must have been feeling desperate.* I try to flip it on its ear and say, *Okay, what they did is really crappy, but what would make a person do that? Imagine how they're feeling.*

Again, it's easy to judge, but what a great opportunity that can be to talk to your kids about looking at the other point of view—a great opportunity to teach your kids to have empathy.

IT'S ALWAYS BETTER TO TALK ABOUT IT

The boys and I live in an insulated, fairly wealthy, and—I'm embarrassed to say—segregated area, but I make sure we go outside of it. I take my children downtown and show them how to volunteer and be part of the whole city, not just our small part of it. I don't want them to think the entire world is like their neighborhood. We are fortunate to live in a nice area. I want them to understand that.

In my view, this is especially important as they get ready to go out on their own. I don't want them to assume that their housing options will be in a neighborhood like this one. I want them to understand why we're here—that I chose this place because of the school system—and that they're going to need to make other choices when they're no longer living here. I want them to know that all choices have consequences. They may want a certain career that doesn't pay particularly well, for example. They need to be able to think that through and make that choice with their eyes open.

This also means they need to make choices about the small things as well as the big ones, and exposing them to things that aren't a part of their daily lives is my way of preparing them to do this. I was never the kind of parent who was quick to turn off the TV or get the kids out of the room when something came on that was problematic in some way. If I thought it was something the kids might benefit from seeing or hearing, I let them stay in the room and explained it to them.

Actually, the kids and I have a running joke that I'm the world's worst movie picker. The problem is that I love all movies. I like everything. I'll watch almost anything. Of course, what this means is that there have been plenty of times when we've settled in for family movie night—and this was happening even when they were very young, back when I was still married—and something would come on that I hadn't anticipated. "What are we *watching?*" one of them would inevitably ask.

Once, I rented *Into the Wild* for family movie night. It's the story of a very bright boy who chooses to turn down a college scholarship, sell all his possessions, and go out, well, into the wild, as the title says. He hikes out into the wilderness, going off on a personal journey. So far, so good.

Somewhere in the middle of the movie, the protagonist is in the woods and comes upon a quarry where there's a group of young people swimming and dancing around. One was a beautiful, naked girl. All of a sudden Henry asked, "What are we watching?" I could see that he was embarrassed by what was on the screen. I stopped the movie and thought, *Okay, I didn't see this coming, but there's no reason to panic.*

"Here's the thing," I said. "There are people all over the world who have different traditions and ways of doing things. She's a free spirit. This is how she does it. It's not the way we behave, but everyone's different. And you never know who or what you'll encounter when you're off on a journey, when you're traveling like he is."

Okay, fine. We started the movie again. What I didn't realize before renting it was that the main character encounters all kinds of situations and then ultimately—more than three hours into the movie—runs out of food, eats poisonous berries, and dies. It's pretty horrific, and probably not what I would have chosen for my kids to watch.

But in some way, it was okay. This character died because he didn't prepare adequately. It was a good lesson about the possible consequences of a choice that someone makes.

"It is easy, when you are young, to believe that what you desire is no less than what you deserve, to assume that if you want something badly enough, it is your God-given right to have it."

—JON KRAKAUER, *INTO THE WILD*

Still, the kids were crying and upset about him dying, and they were asking me why I'd chosen the movie. Especially since I'd already told them that it was based on a true story. I didn't have the heart to launch into the life lesson—the need to prepare, the need to make good choices, and the consequences of making bad decisions. I ended up just saying that I was sorry, that I hadn't known how it ended. "Okay, Mom," said George at last.

So my choice of that movie wasn't particularly well thought out. But I don't like turning back. I feel that once we're in, we're in. That there are other ways to deal with things like making a poor choice of movie besides just turning it off because it contains something offensive, sad, or inexplicable. I'd prefer to stop and talk about whatever it is and then continue on rather than cut off the conversation.

There are myriad other things in the world your kids will encounter that will be difficult to explain. Homelessness, people getting sick, none of this is easy to talk about. Even in our insulated community, bad things happen. At some point in their life, everyone's going to experience something difficult.

When my father was diagnosed with cancer, I tried to be strong around my boys. But there came a day I couldn't do that anymore. When this happened, I couldn't be the leader of the family. I needed to be a person—a daughter—someone who didn't want her father to die. George came in that day and found me sobbing, and he asked me what was wrong. I said, "I don't want my dad to die. I love him so much." I think George was both frightened and horrified, seeing me like that, but when I looked at him, I could see the empathy and understanding in his face. He was thinking, *Oh, my gosh, I get it. I wouldn't want my dad to die, either.*

GOING THE EXTRA MILE

The example I gave of my father's diagnosis was obviously close to home; it was something that affected me personally. But empathy needs to go beyond just things that affect us personally. Here again, too often, we think it's all about us. We hear about a project and want to get our kids involved. "Let's do a Habitat for Humanity house," we might say, when in truth, Habitat for Humanity may not be where your kid wants to be. A lot of churches and schools promote various missions, but if you *make* your kids participate, the experience (and what they learn from it) may not be genuine, because it's your choice, not theirs.

On the other hand, any experience that puts your kids in a place that isn't their normal, safe zone is valuable.

When George was twelve years old, he went with a group of other kids to Kingston, Jamaica. A friend of mine named Jeffrey Wenzler runs a nonprofit organization called Pivotal Direction that teaches leadership skills to teens; he started it after watching his brother die of a drug overdose when he was a teenager. Jeffrey later wrote a fantastic book about it called *The Pivotal Life*, which has now been made into a documentary. He takes kids on leadership trips to Jamaica and Guatemala. In Kingston, the kids literally live in a landfill alongside the city's poorest residents. They work in an orphanage, a school, and a home for the dying.

The kids are there for just seven to fourteen days, but for many, it's a life-altering experience.

George really wanted to go. I don't know what I was thinking at the time! He had barely even been on an airplane. We'd never gone on a family trip before, but here I was, letting George go off to live in a landfill.

And then I started getting the pictures he was sending me from Jamaica. George holding small children in the landfill. George with a man in his nineties, having a conversation together at the hospice. And I realized that the George I was seeing in these photos wasn't the same George who'd left home only days before.

Of course, that new, mature, dynamic person didn't last. He came home, and eventually, he went back to being the same old George. But I know that somewhere in the vault of his brain, that experience is still there, and that other George lives on. If we can all try and bring out that other person in our kids, even in small ways, such as holding the door for someone at the grocery store, then we'll let them see that they can make a difference in the world.

George at the airport leaving for Jamaica

George with one of the schoolchildren

It wasn't that I expected George to come home and start his own nonprofit or anything like that, especially as he was the youngest kid who'd ever gone on the trip. But some of the older kids did. One came home and started a nonprofit that collects extra school supplies at the end of the school year and distributes them to other schools that need them. Another kid started a clean water project. There are a lot of neat things that have started as a result of this group, and while George was too young to have gone that route, the experience still left an imprint on him, and I'm convinced that it did because it was something that he chose to do, rather than something I chose for him.

My feelings about it were mixed. Part of me was thinking, *Gosh, how cool would it be to be able to keep him in this moment for as long as possible?* But I had also experienced a lot of fear around the trip. Jeffrey and the kids stayed at a convent inside the landfill with armed guards around the place twenty-four hours a day. Given this, I think some people questioned my decision to let George go there. My reaction to this? "Whatever." Other people's judgment has never stopped me from doing too many things.

ASK THE QUESTIONS

As you're thinking about stepping back and letting your kids develop empathy, it's helpful to ask them questions.

I've found that it's better to ask what's going on rather than make assumptions. Sometimes, our asking questions is what helps give them the answer—helps them articulate something that only they can feel.

Once when Henry was quite young, someone was bullying him. The kid kept telling Henry, "I'm going to beat your face in." When I heard that, I asked Henry if he wanted to invite the kid over.

"Are you out of your mind, Mom?" he said. "I don't want him over at my house!"

"Do you think that he's lonely?" I countered. "Do you think he's bullying you because he doesn't have any friends? That this is his way of communicating with you?"

I was just trying to get Henry to ask himself the questions—to ask why this kid was behaving that way. If you can get to the *why* of things, you can often feel empathy for the other person. People don't go around shooting each other or robbing banks because it's fun. They do it because they're scared, upset, hurt—any number of things could have contributed to their behavior. I'm not ignorant enough to think that we're going to stop all of that, but when I bring it back to my own children and to them going out into the world, I just want them to think about the situation and others' behavior. If they're around somebody who's behaving a certain way, I want my kids to ask why that person might be behaving the way they are. If someone's freaking out in a bar, I want my kids to think about why they're doing it. Then I want them to remove themselves from the situation or try to diffuse it, whatever seems best.

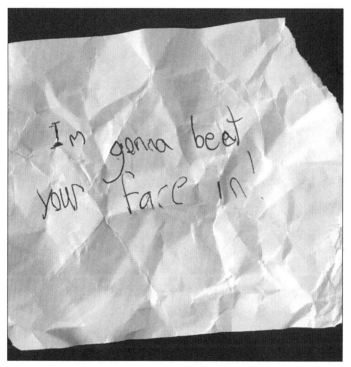

Note from the playground bully

Here's what I tell them: If you start to think about other people more than yourself, as opposed to merely thinking that they're making you angry, then maybe you're going to have a little more insight into the situation. I think that the former reaction is more natural, but the latter is more constructive.

Hopefully, empathy is something that your kid can pack in their mental and emotional suitcase as they prepare to leave home. But there's something else they have to pack, too, and it's a lot more basic than empathy.

CHAPTER FOUR

TEACHING THE BASICS

———

I say "teaching the basics," but these aren't things that parents usually think about teaching their kids. However, they *are* things that kids probably don't know how to do. Kids don't even know that some of these things exist, or that they're important. You can ease the transition a lot—and possibly avoid some of the panicked calls you'll be getting once your kids are living on their own—by going over these areas with them.

MANAGING TIME

As I've mentioned before, I'd never be anywhere at the right time if I didn't write my appointments down in a whole lot of places. They're on my phone, on a piece of paper in my purse, on a pad of paper on my kitchen counter, and on another pad of paper that's next to my bed. I have notes everywhere telling me what I'm going to do that day. I have a list for the grocery store, I have a list for what errands I need to run, I have a list for what I'm going to do for work over the course of the next month and even what I'm planning on doing in general. I have tons of lists.

Even with me setting this example, for the longest time, Henry had no calendar. Schools pass out little planners, and kids are supposed to write their homework assignments in them. Henry never wrote anything down, which is why many of his assignments didn't get handed in.

I don't think Henry's ever given a lot of thought to the cause-and-effect involved in planning time and activities. The only way he's been able to begin to master any kind of organization is by having a lot of commitments that are important to him. He has a job, he has his climbing team and his climbing group, and he has school, and he wants to show up for those activities, so he's slowly beginning to understand that the only way he can do it all is to get a grip on time management.

I don't think that you have to teach your kids to be ultra-compulsive, but you do need to help them find a system they'll actually use for managing their time. Everyone's got a smartphone, and it's not that difficult to punch in an appointment or reminder. At the very least, we can teach our kids to do that. (Better yet, they can probably teach us to do it. I mean, I think most of our kids are much more tech-savvy than we are. We can give them the concept; they can give us the process.)

It's not just about the logistics of time management, though. It's about the importance of doing it—what values are attached to it. In essence, missing an appointment or not showing up for it on time is a sign of disrespect for the other people involved. Yes, everybody's late sometimes, and people apologize and move on. But if you consistently disregard someone else's time, you're sending them a pretty strong message that you don't care that much about them, their priorities, or their resources.

I don't know that anyone ever said those words to me as a kid. I think that it was something I had to learn over time.

George is a little more naturally organized than his brother. He keeps a calendar and always seems know where he's supposed to be. I don't ever wonder if he's going to remember to go to lacrosse practice, for example. But up until recently, I would have to frequently check in with Henry.

He got better after I spent a lot of time showing him how to keep a calendar and pay attention to it.

That was a lesson for me. For some kids, parents modeling certain behaviors is enough. Other kids you have to stay with step-by-step until they figure out that this really *is* important. Because it is. We all know adults who don't respect anyone else's time, who don't care about courtesy, who miss appointments. This behavior can be devastating to them, either in their careers or in other ways. A lot of negative things happen if you don't make sure you do what you're supposed to do, if you don't follow through on the commitments you've made.

SETTING GOALS

I've always been pretty goal-oriented. I'm constantly reminding my kids, "You need to have a goal. If you're not intentionally trying to get somewhere, you're never going to get anywhere." But the reality is that kids don't automatically know about setting goals. They don't even necessarily know what goals are.

This means you have to start with teaching kids the basics about setting goals. A goal doesn't have to be anything big, anything extraordinary. The important thing is that the goal is tangible. You have to be able to know when you've achieved it. I always encourage the boys to write their goals down. Are you trying to get an A in your government class? What is the process for reaching that goal? What are the steps involved in making that happen? Do you just need to show up at school? Study more? What's the plan?

Asking these questions is good way to accomplish what needs to be done, and it's so rewarding to reach goals. Every one of our kids should be able to feel that pleasure and sense of accomplishment.

When you start early enough, you build up to the ability to reach better and higher goals. If I set a goal to save twenty-five dollars when I am fifteen years old and reach that goal, then I'm going to be a lot more successful when my goal is to save for a down payment for my first house. That's because I know what it was like to try and save, and what sacrifices I had to make. Maybe I wasn't able to go to a movie on the weekend because I had to keep saving my money. Now, I'm not able to go on a trip because I'm saving my money for the house. Whatever it is, I understand the concept.

Henry has his first job now, and he loves to buy expensive climbing gear. It's important to me that when he buys gear, he understands that it is a choice—that in choosing to spend his money in that way, he's also choosing to *not* spend it in another way. "Henry," I've often said, "if you keep buying all that gear, you aren't going to have any money when you want to go on this trip," or, "You're not going to have money saved up for college if you don't put aside some money from each paycheck." We talk a lot about his goals for saving money and his goals for other things. Ultimately, it's Henry's money, Henry's job, and so it's Henry's choice. But so are the consequences; Henry is actually very responsible for the average high school senior. He's been working for almost a year and a half, his employer loves him because he's very dependable, and although he buys a lot of expensive gear, he's still managing to save some money for college.

From the beginning, George saved every penny he had. When he was young, he wanted to buy a 3D game that cost $270. He saved his money and bought it. He had the goal of buying it, he put together a plan for achieving his goal, and he succeeded. I was impressed with the process. He totally understood what he was doing. I didn't have to worry about how he was spending his money: I knew he had saved it with the intention of spending it on the game.

Henry working at Sendik's Food Market

KEEPING A CALENDAR

A school planner works for homework assignments, but time management requires more than that. Even adults have a lot of trouble with time management. We all know someone who's chronically late. We all know someone who says, "I have to do some paperwork, then the laundry, then go to the store, then bake a lasagna..." It just goes on and on and on. *Wait a second,* I've found myself thinking. *When exactly are you doing all that?* A lot of people aren't realistic about the number of events, appointments, and tasks that they can fit into their schedules.

The easiest way to avoid overscheduling is to calendar everything—to treat everything as an appointment. If you need to schedule your lunch, schedule it in as an appointment. You think it's not going to take very long, but in my experience, everything takes about twice as much time as you think it will.

I have a friend who is a brilliant man, but he's also over-zealous (and unrealistic) about what he wants to do every day. He'd sometimes call me at five o'clock and he'd say, "Okay, so we're going to have dinner later, right?"

"Yeah, great," I'd say.

Then he'd say, "So I think first I'm going to go and do a quick workout at the gym. Then I'm going to take a shower and run to the bookstore. After that, I'll head to the grocery store and buy some steaks. Before I cook, though, I'm going to spend a little time clearing out that space in the garage." I would already be starting to say something when he'd add, "Then I'll fire up the grill."

There was only one possible response. "Which day is it that we're having dinner, today or tomorrow?"

The grill would get fired up at 10 pm and I'd be angry (not to mention hungry!). I interpreted this as his disrespecting my time and not caring about doing anything with me. I was always offended. He wasn't an idiot. He *knew* he couldn't do everything on that list. And I was feeling that I came last.

The kids saw all of this, and I said to them, "You guys, you're going do the same thing if you don't start writing down how much stuff you can do at a time. Because you can't get it all done." I wanted my kids to understand that they could do one or maybe two things in two hours, not eight or ten things.

I think that if kids aren't realistic about what can get done, it's easy for them to get overwhelmed. That's where I've always found calendars to be helpful. Instead of thinking, *I'll never get all of this done,* you can say, *This needs to be done Wednesday, and that can wait until Friday.* There's a certain sense of comfort and relief that comes with knowing that it's all planned out. It allows you to concentrate on one thing and always be present in the here and now. There's a significant amount of peace that comes with knowing that things are under control.

After the whole debacle during which Henry didn't hand in his homework for two weeks, his father and I weren't quite sure we understood what was happening for him. We asked Henry if he might want to talk to a counselor, and he said, "Sure," partly, I suspect, because Henry actually loves to talk to adults.

We set up the first appointment for him, but as you've probably gathered, I'm a big fan of letting him take the reins. "You're in charge from here on out," I told him. "If you want to talk to her again, then you have to set up the appointment and be responsible for it." He set up another appointment. He and his counselor were talking about his readiness for college and exploring whether he might want to take a gap year. The plan for his next appointment was to write up a proposal for a gap year, in case he wanted to do that.

So there he was, in charge. He set up a second appointment with the counselor. And it's worth noting that each appointment cost $200. That's a lot of money for one hour. He knew that, and he knew that his dad and I were going to be paying for the sessions. So what happened?

He forgot the appointment. He just didn't show up. Of course, the office didn't call Henry; they called me. "Hi, this is the North Shore Center. We're wondering if Henry is coming to his appointment?"

Oops. I turned to him. "What are you doing, Henry? Why are you here?"

"Oh, my God!" he exclaimed. "I forgot!"

Then, of course, the whole thing blew up. "Okay," I said. "Then you can pay for it. You can't *just forget*. There's a lot going on here!" I started ticking things off on my fingers. "One, we've talked about the calendar. Two, we've talked about disrespecting people's time. Three, we've talked about the money it would cost. This is a problem on so many levels!" Both his dad and I felt that he should pay for it, and that he should be the one to call and remedy the situation.

What I have to point out here is that Henry is a smart kid who's also very nice. People at his job love him. He just got a promotion. But he's a normal kid. He's a normal kid who didn't write his appointment on his calendar. He's never missed an appointment since then. The money made it real. He doesn't want to spend a week and a half's worth of wages paying for a missed appointment.

FAILURE *IS* AN OPTION

The scenario I described above can be very hard on parents. Following through is very difficult. I felt sorry for him. *Poor Henry,* I thought. *He has to work for a week and a half to pay for that.* But the reality was that he was never going to learn that lesson otherwise. Never.

I've mentioned this before, but kids are going to screw up, out there in the world. They're going to make mistakes. They're going to fail. So it's useful to give them the opportunity to make the mistakes and learn from them at home, before they go out in the world and the consequences are heavier. "No matter," wrote Samuel Beckett. "Try again. Fail again. Fail better." If we can give our kids the experience of failing and then failing better, they'll be on their way to being a bigger success.

THE TAXMAN COMETH

The lesson that Henry learned had to do with calendars and appointments, but it also had to do with money. People place a monetary value on their time. The real problem in managing money, I think, is that money is so abstract.

I'm a strong believer in kids having a job before they leave home. I had a job from the time I turned sixteen. If you have a job, you have a paycheck. If you have a paycheck, you have a bank account. If you have a bank account, you have a W2 form. If you have a W2 form, you have to fill out a tax return.

Henry didn't have to fill out a tax return this year, but he will next year, and his college financial-aid forms required copies of his W2 forms. He was startled and asked, "Well, was I supposed to fill out a tax return?" I told him that he hadn't made enough that year to file, but that he'd have to the following year. It wasn't a long conversation, but it was a necessary one. How else would he know?

The truth is that kids have no idea. They don't know at what point they have to start paying taxes, they don't know what forms to use, and they don't know what paperwork they'll need. We had a conversation about the EZ form and what it looks like, and if we hadn't, he'd have had no clue as to how to fill it out. Henry would just never have filled out a tax form at all if I hadn't brought it up with him and taught him the need to fill out a tax form if you make more than certain amount of money in a year.

I think it's important to put the information in front of kids. Go through it with them so that they understand that when they get their first job, they'll need to fill out a form asking about exemptions (where their employer takes money out in advance) and make sure there's enough money to pay their taxes, that sort of thing. I think, again, that's a pretty basic conversation, but when it comes to tax time, a lot of young people just panic. (Frankly, I panic too, sometimes. Thank God for my accountant!)

What I remember from tax time when I was kid is hearing my sister say, "Oh, my God. Stay away from Mom and Dad. Like, they're super-cranky!" That wasn't exactly the greatest introduction to filing income taxes. And then, when I got my first job in high school, my parents took the paperwork and did my tax form for me. All I had to do was sign where they told me to sign. So I had to figure it all out on my own once I moved away from home. It would have been helpful for me to have the confidence of already knowing.

MANAGING MONEY

None of this is rocket science. It's all simply activities and behaviors that you have to perform as an adult just to get through the day. But what we forget—because we've done all this tedious paperwork for so many years—is that no one is born knowing about this stuff. If you don't teach it to your kids, they won't learn it.

Many kids own cars while they're still in high school. Henry has one, too. But I made him find out how much he needed to pay for insurance and send in the insurance information for his car. It would have been easier for me to do it, but I wanted him to see how much paperwork is involved in daily life. We can't expect kids to just magically know everything that has to be done.

Many—if not most—kids live in college dorms when they're freshmen, and many of them move out into an apartment during their sophomore year. When they think about having an apartment, they get all excited. They think about how to decorate the apartment, they think about the fun of having pizzas delivered, and they think about buying a cool sound system. What they *don't* think about is how to get the apartment in the first place. They don't know what's on a rental application. They certainly don't know that it's difficult to get an apartment if they don't have any credit, and that there's no such thing as instant credit.

The obvious answer is for your kid to get their first credit card when they're still living at home, or right when they turn eighteen. Then they'll have some sort of credit established before they apply to rent a place.

Your kid's first credit card comes with its own set of possible problems, of course. A lot of people, no matter what their age, run up amazing balances on their first credit card. Why not? It feels like free money. And I won't lie to you; it's going to be tempting for your child to do the same thing. It's going to be up to you to make it clear that there's no such thing as free money, ever. And, good or bad, your credit score follows you around, as we parents are only too aware.

Once you start talking about money, the opportunities for life lessons start flowing, one following the next: Here's what a credit report looks like. (I don't think that any kids see a credit report while they're under their parents' roof. This could be time well spent.) Here's how to check your credit. Never put anything on your card that you can't pay off in a month. Lessons like that.

I went with Henry to buy his first car. The plan was for him to pay for his gas and also pay fifty dollars a month toward the car itself. I made sure that he was with me for the whole process, including deciding what to buy, how to negotiate, all of it. We applied for credit—in my name—and naturally, my credit score report was pulled.

There was a problem with the report.

What I eventually learned was disturbing. My mortgage company had failed to report a payment, causing my score to go down by over one hundred points. I had it fixed, of course, but in the meantime, we had to buy the car—and my score meant that the interest rate we were offered was sky-high.

I was extremely upset. There we were, sitting at the car dealership, and I was trying to understand the situation. I was making calls and asking questions, and meanwhile Henry was on *his* phone, just playing around. He wasn't even listening. I tried telling him how serious the situation was, and he remained indifferent. "I don't know," he said. "Whatever. It's your problem."

"No, it's not," I said. "Now the payment's going to be $30 higher every month and that affects you, because you're paying for part of it. You'll be paying more."

A lot of people would just go buy the car, bring it home, and hand the keys to their son. I don't believe in that. I think that being part of the process is essential. He ended up learning a lot that day. He learned to check his credit report, check to see if anything is wrong, and fix it if there is. I made him do the math. Thirty dollars over the course of a sixty-month loan adds up to $1,800. That's a lot of climbing gear!

Recently, I was at lunch with a group of women, and I was talking about writing this book. "Hey," I said. "I'm curious if any of you have any stories about kids and money management you want to share."

One of them immediately volunteered. Her daughter, a very bright girl in medical school, was carrying a staggering number of student loans. She was coasting along on the assumption that once she was a doctor, she'd be making a lot of money, so she could spend whatever she needed to now. She opened credit card after credit card at whatever interest rate was being offered. However, the more credit card loans she got, the less she was able to pay them. They just kept racking up and were getting worse and worse. Finally, she had no money. She couldn't pay anyone.

When she brought herself to tell her parents and ask for help, my friend was astonished. How could this have happened? She shook her head as she told me the story. "I just had no idea that this could happen to my daughter, who is a smart, smart girl. Clearly, we didn't tell her something. Clearly, there's a message that we missed giving her, because we never dreamed in a million years that this would happen to her. If I had ever thought that there was something I could have told her to prevent this from happening, I would have told her."

So what should we do? Should the parents step in, or allow the child to fail? These parents helped their daughter formulate a plan to get out of debt. The thing that struck me the most, however, was how surprised her mom was. This is a good example of how we *assume* that our kids can just figure these things out. They can't.

Another concept that's abstract for kids is health insurance. A lot of kids are on their parents' health insurance, and they can stay on it until they're twenty-six, but I think it's very helpful if kids understand from the start the process of choosing and obtaining health insurance. Especially now. The health insurance industry is changing so much that it's essential for them to understand how those changes affect them.

Whenever we're at the doctor's office, again, I make my kids part of the process. "Here's the insurance card, and we have to make a co-pay that goes toward our deductible. Our deductible is three thousand dollars per person, but a maximum of six thousand dollars for our family." I try to explain the basics of health insurance so that they understand it, because then they're not just walking into the doctor's office and saying, "Yeah, no worries. Mom's got insurance." Even when I'm sitting down to pay medical bills, I show them the bills.

George had a very significant accident a few years ago, when he was fourteen. He was standing on a boathouse that collapsed under him. He was seriously injured. He broke four bones in his foot, tore a tendon on the side of his leg, and punctured the back of his head. He couldn't walk for almost five months and had to endure a significant surgery. There were a lot of medical bills, it was a major endeavor sorting it all out, and I made George participate in the process. Up until then, he'd always been the kind of kid who wanted to go to the doctor's office to be checked out for the smallest scratch. I wanted him to see both the cost and the paperwork involved in any medical intervention.

Car insurance is another thorny issue. Henry drives, and George is taking driver's education. And while I actually pay for Henry's insurance, he pays a certain amount every month that is his contribution toward car payments, insurance, and maintenance/repairs. But I don't let him off the hook for the paperwork, because he needs to know all the things involved in operating a car.

All of this comes back to the same theme. We assume our kids will automatically know what they have to do and understand the process involved in doing it. And when we find out that they don't, this can have grown into a very expensive problem to fix.

A lot of schools have some sort of a class that teaches essential finances for living in which students do basic household accounting, savings, retirement finances, and filling out tax forms. If your kids can take that class at their high school, it's a great preparation for what awaits them. It will reinforce what you're teaching at home and show them that it's not just you being obsessive about specifics, but that those specifics are essential for a well-regulated life.

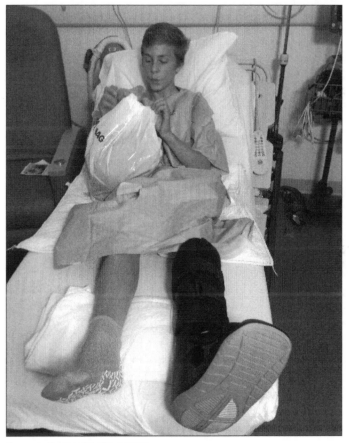

George in the hospital after surgery

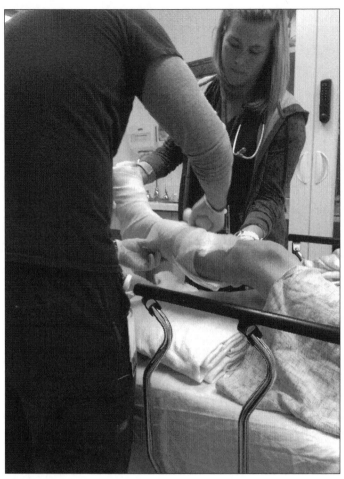

Trauma center with George

OPEN YOUR MAIL!

Bills are another major issue. I've heard so many stories—an unbelievable number of stories—of young people not wanting to face what's come in the mail. They don't want to see it, so they don't open the mail, and their bills pile up. There's some magical thinking involved. *If I don't see it, I don't have to pay it.*

I think if you show your kids once or twice the penalties for *not* paying your bills on time, or the interest that accrues when you wait to pay bills, it might be enough to scare them. We can only hope so. In any case, they'll realize it pretty quickly once it starts happening. A good example always helps: Three credit card late fees at $39 each equals $117; $117 *could* have equaled one cute J. Crew top or two concert tickets!

Nothing in that pile of mail is scarier than things will get if a debt collector gets involved. Better to just get it over with.

BUDGETING

Budgeting is especially hard for kids to understand. First of all, they don't think much into the future. Secondly, they're willing to budget, but only for the things that are sexy and fun, like a new car or a new dress. They're not as interested in budgeting for the electric bill.

It's very easy when you see your kids suffering, even if it's only a little, to want to hand them ten dollars, because ten dollars to you and me might not be a very big deal. Your kid's crying because they can't have the video game, or they can't go to a movie with their friends, because they don't have the money. Whatever it is, it's easy to just hand them the money.

But when you're considering doing that, remember that very soon, handouts from their parents won't be an option for them, and they're not going to know what to do out in the real world when they don't have the money. They're not going to know how to plan ahead so that they *do* have it when they need to spend it.

Henry makes a decent amount of money, three or four hundred dollars every two weeks, and he could have thousands of dollars saved already. Instead, he likes to buy climbing gear, which is very expensive. He promises that he's going to save for college "sometime," but doesn't have a plan for when said savings will take place.

We've had innumerable discussions about budgeting and saving. I think that it's reasonable for him to do whatever he wants to with 25 percent of his paycheck, and then the other 75 percent should go in the bank for college and/or whatever else is needed. Henry has a bank account, and he does save money, but spending can be a slippery slope. Unless I'm keeping an eye on it, his money doesn't always go in the bank. Still, it's good for him to see what the percentages should be...and how difficult it is to live within that budget. George doesn't have a job, but he's pretty good about saving for something he wants. Though inevitably, even for George, there are times when he doesn't have any money.

Of course, right now, the consequences of not budgeting aren't too terrible. If a kid can't go to a movie because they don't have the money, that's not the end of the world. But when you're living on your own and you have no money, and you can't pay your bills, and you're getting stressed out because college is already stressful, and you have to concentrate on turning in your homework and the challenges of getting along with your peers, and you're homesick, and then on top of it all, suddenly you can't pay for anything, then life becomes a disaster. Your room-mates are asking for your portion of the rent, and you don't have any food. You're starving, and you're getting crankier by the second. Then you're thinking, *What am I going to do? I'm screwed.*

When that happens, there are a couple of options. You can call your parents. You could borrow money from someone, which is the worst option because you're continuing that cycle. You just have to figure out a way to get through it, and then make sure it doesn't happen again.

When I first got divorced, we went through some very difficult financial times. I remember being almost broke, which was especially difficult because we were living in pretty affluent area. My children were nine and eleven at the time, and I didn't want them to feel any of the pressure I was feeling. But the truth is that I was in a complete state of panic every day, and especially every night. I had no idea what I would do. Every single day, I woke up after barely sleeping the night before, and from morning to night, I was frightened. How was I going to buy food? How could I continue to put gas in the car, pay the rent, manage to keep life ticking over for us? I didn't have any idea.

I did all the things I mentioned earlier. I sold everything I could, even objects and mementos that were meaningful to me. I sat down and made a realistic budget. I wrote down everything that I had to pay for every month. Then I looked at it and asked myself, *Okay, where can I cut? I don't need this. I don't need that. How do we cut down on the food? We don't need to eat out.* I thought hard about my budget and then I thought, *Okay, well, I might need a second job.* I had to figure out how to make some money.

When push comes to shove, what we're talking about here is basic math. You just have to figure out how to make it work. If you don't have any money, you need to get more money. You need to work more, or you need to spend less, or both. You can't make something out of nothing, so your plan has to involve more than just juggling numbers around. Making a viable plan means changing the way you're doing things.

Talking to your kids about a budget and about how *you* budget is essential. They'll emulate you in a lot of the things you do, even though they'd never admit it. They want to be completely, totally different from you most of the time, but they're watching you. So let them see you pay the bills. Let them see you fill out paperwork.

Your budgeting abilities will rub off on your kids. And even when they're disappointed at not being able to buy something, they'll have a glimmer of understanding as to why. One of my kids recently asked for a new pair of fancy shoes. "You know what?" I said. "We can buy them, but not right this second. I just can't spend the money right now." It's important that they hear those words sometimes, so that they understand that you have a budget and you're sticking to it.

You can involve them in the choices you make as well, and model decision-making for them. For example, I might say, "We spend $150 or $200 a week on groceries, and that's all that's budgeted for. We can go out to eat once this week, but we won't have dessert more than once if we do that. Which do you want to do?" You don't have to be talking about it constantly, but your kids need to know that there is a plan in place, and everyone has to be on board with it.

MANAGING MINDS AND BODIES

So once we have the money under control, there's still the question of health, especially mental health. How can I help my kids take care of themselves once they're gone? How will I know that this new experience isn't affecting them adversely, causing anxiety or depression? Fortunately, there's more discussion around mental health now than there ever was when we were younger.

Hopefully, kids these days are starting to understand that seeing a counselor doesn't mean that they're sick or mentally imbalanced. It's just a healthy thing to do. Bouncing ideas off someone else is actually a sign of being super-well adjusted. I think that the stigma around seeking out professional help is going away and that, more and more, kids understand that anyone can benefit from counseling at some point in their lives. Certainly, there's less of a stigma around it for my kids' generation than there was for mine.

Almost everyone has a friend—or at least somebody that they know of—who has had a deeper mental health issue, like depression or anxiety. Because the conversation is more in the open now, it's more possible for them to get help—or for a friend to refer them.

I was actually just talking with a young woman who's the receptionist in my office. We were talking about Planned Parenthood, and she mentioned that the agency offers mental health resources, which I thought was interesting. I'm not sure everyone knows that, and they should. Making a list of the agencies in your area that offer different kinds of physical and mental health support is a great way to start the conversation with your kids. Once they've chosen their next stop—college or gap year or whatever—sit down with them and list the agencies available to help them or someone they know in the area. It will give them somewhere to turn when they need help.

Kids need to know that *not* getting help can be detrimental. I know people who have committed suicide, and know that sometimes it's the people who seem the most pulled together and cheerful who are depressed or in pain. People you'd never think are struggling with mental illness, people who light up the room when they come into it.

A very close friend of mine was one of these people, and she ended up hanging herself. That absolutely shook me to the core. When something like that happens, it affects everyone around the person. I went to a counselor for a while after that event. I also resolved to encourage my boys to see a therapist if something ever happened to one of their friends or classmates, or anytime they felt they need to talk something out. It didn't have to be a significant event, I told them.

It's good for you to be aware of your own mental health, and it's important that your kids check in with you and themselves about their own. You can't necessarily prevent people from doing dreadful things, but you can be a good friend and aware of their problems and anxieties. You can also know how to find resources if you, or someone you care about, needs them.

I've probably asked my kids at least fifty times, "Do you want to go to a counselor? Are you feeling anxious? Are you sad?" George says all the time, "School is really stressful," and I know that's true. The boys go to an extremely difficult school. It's a school that puts a lot of pressure on the students, and many of them take high-intensity AP classes. Sometimes, I think that when kids are pushed to do more and more, they're going to snap at some point. So kids absolutely need to know about these resources.

In an earlier chapter, we talked about having conversations with your kids before an emergency arises during which they'll need to act. This is even more important when you're looking at potential mental health issues. Talking about these ahead of time is better than having your kid come home in shock because a classmate has intentionally overdosed.

One of the things that I think creates a good dialogue is discussing certain words and what they mean to both you and to your kid. When your kid says, "I'm so stressed out," does that mean "I'm nervous about my upcoming test or game," or does it mean "The whole world is on top of me and I have no way out?" Knowing each other's vocabulary means it's easier to know when to get help.

And, again, being prepared is the best thing you can do for your kids' mental and physical health. They're going to be attending parties. They're going to be around other kids who are doing unhealthy things. They may do unhealthy things themselves, like drink too much or take too many drugs. Support them by giving them solutions to the problematic or dangerous situations that are bound to arise. Have the Uber app on their phone, even if you have to set them up with your credit card. We're probably all in agreement that we don't want our kid getting into a car and driving and hitting somebody and then forever having that decision affect their life and the life of the person they injured.

There are special problems for parents of daughters. Imagine your daughter out at a bar when one of the girls says, "Don't worry about me. I'm going to go home with my new friend, Jim." Typically, the other girls will say, "Okay, see you later." If you've already had a conversation about safety with your daughter, then she'll be better able to cope, she'll understand that letting her friend leave with somebody is not doing that friend any favors, and that her friend may end up having sex (consensual or nonconsensual), which she may later regret. Or she could get hurt. Or she could be killed. And there's no one on Earth who wants that on their conscience.

Whether you have a son or a daughter, it's important for them to understand that being a good friend means thinking ahead sometimes. So you need to have the conversation about what might happen, and ask the questions: How would you approach a friend who's leaving with a stranger? What can you say to her to change her mind? How else can you stop her?

Our kids absolutely need to talk about this before it happens. They need to talk with us, and they need to talk with their network of friends about what to do when some of these situations arise. Those conversations have to take place ahead of time, because kids are never going to make good, well-thought-through decisions in the moment. No one does!

When my best friend's daughter, Hannah, went away to UCLA, I gave her my phone number and told her she could call me, no matter what happened, at any time, day or night. I wanted to be a point person for her—someone she could turn to in a crisis. Of course, she could call her parents or somebody else as well, but I just wanted to make it clear that she could also call me, and I wouldn't judge anything. I'd be there to help her. As a parent, if you could be that person for someone else's child, I think it's nice to offer that child the option. Doing so might just save their life if, for some reason, they don't want to call their own parents.

I actually hope that there's someone who will make that same offer to Henry and George. The boys' friends' parents are fantastic, and I would feel so grateful if any one of them said to the boys, "Call us anytime." It's good to have a community of people there to look after and care about our kids. It truly does take a village.

In terms of thinking about your kids' bodies, it's essential that they leave your home both valuing and protecting them. It's important to have a discussion about respecting their own bodies and those of other kids. I don't remember having that conversation with my parents. For me and the boys, the discussion started early, when the boys were ten and twelve. Which isn't to say that it's not ongoing!

Whenever the opportunity presents itself to have the conversation about respect again, maybe looking at things from a slightly difference angle, I take it. I suggest that you take it, too. Then you can just keep the door open and keep the conversation going.

When the kids were younger, they didn't have their own laptops. We used a family desktop that we all shared, and I had my own personal laptop. I just opened it one day, and I'm not sure why I happened to look at the browser history, but I did, and was a little shocked to see what was there. It was a whole succession of pornography sites. Pages and pages of them.

I walked into the family room where George and Henry were watching TV, and I asked who had been using my laptop. Henry volunteered right away: "I was. I'm sorry." He was noticeably embarrassed and worried about my reaction. I invited him to come upstairs so we could talk in private. "Okay," I said, "it's totally normal that you looked at these sites. I don't know how you got to them, but it's not abnormal that you wanted to, or that you were curious about them. But you know this isn't how I want you to view women. This isn't a way of respecting or valuing women." We had a conversation about it then, and that felt good, but it's a discussion that's never truly over. As you move forward, the shape of the conversation may change, but it's important to continue it. This isn't the sort of thing that you can say once and then just forget.

When I told my best friend Lisa about Henry's perusal of porn sites, she gave me a book called *What's Going On Down There?* That was a godsend. What a book! Henry acted like I'd given him a winning lottery ticket. He was twelve years old, and I'd given him a book about every aspect of puberty, one that gets into the nitty-gritty of everything. Amazingly, he read that book start to finish in a day. It's a pretty long book.

What this showed me is that Henry wanted the knowledge. Yes, maybe he wanted to watch porn, but I think what he *really* wanted was to know more. We still have jokes about the *What's Going On Down There* book, but the idea is for us as parents to be willing to give all the information our kids need. They might not ask us directly, but we need to be sensitive to signs that they want to learn more. Don't worry about offering too much information. Your kid knows exactly how much they want to know, and they'll stop you if you've passed that boundary.

Even with lots of education, when it comes to their bodies, kids going away to college for the first time still have a lot of confusion.

I remember that when I first got to college, there was a lot of whispering about a girl who had herpes. Everyone knew about it, which must have been dreadful for her. I remember being horrified and thinking that I wouldn't have a clue what to do if I were in her place. I just didn't know *anything* about the world of venereal disease. And I would have been embarrassed to ask anybody about it. I wouldn't have known where to go.

Kids need to know that there's on-campus medical care (often for free) for family planning issues, and off-campus there's Planned Parenthood, which offers a lot of services and has a sliding fee scale. I think that perhaps parents are afraid to tell their kids about those services because they don't want it to seem like an invitation or a free pass to unbridled sexual activity. But the alternative is that kids ignore situations that arise and that, if left untreated, can affect their health for the rest of their lives.

MANAGING MEDIA

I wrote earlier about some of the perils inherent in social media. It's not just a kid's issue, either. I see a lot of adults who can't get control of their use of Facebook or LinkedIn, and I think that the truth is that nobody yet knows exactly what the best way to use it all is.

There's not necessarily *any* best way, actually.

It's important to talk with your kids about their social media use. First of all, these sites can represent a tremendous time-suck. Hours can quickly go by when you're on Facebook or Twitter or Snapchat. It's also important to have conversations with your kids about the social interaction aspect. We spend so much time looking at our phones, looking at the computer, looking at the TV that's hooked up to the game that's hooked up to the headphones that are hooked up to the computer, that we lose the knack of having meaningful interactions with our families, friends, and other people in our lives.

George often has headphones on, is hooked up to the computer, and—here's the kicker—he's playing games with friends *who only live blocks away from us.* I don't get the process. I don't see why he doesn't just go over to his friends' houses. And when I talk to him about it, he laughs at me and says that I don't understand. He's right. I don't. I don't think there's any replacement for real face-to-face human interaction, and that's a concept I want my kids to internalize. The technology is adjunct; it isn't a replacement for being with real people.

In business, when I want to get something done, I put down the phone. I don't email. I don't text. I don't do anything on the computer. I make an appointment. I meet face-to-face with somebody because that's where all the business actually gets done. I've even noticed that these face-to-face meetings are coming back into vogue, that people are starting to remember what it's like to *not* use technology as a substitute for human interactions.

So one of your goals in managing media has to be setting some boundaries at home so that when your kids go off to college, they know how to manage their time and usage of social media, gaming, and more.

CHAPTER FIVE

THE NEW HOME(WORK)

———

Once your kid leaves your house, homework isn't just about books anymore. Suddenly, your son or daughter has to manage—or at least comanage—a small household. And while tasks like making the bed seem negligible in the grand scheme of things, they actually aren't. Making the bed, doing the laundry, and organizing stuff teaches a kid to take care of themselves and respect their own space and possessions, as well as those of others.

A WELL-MADE BED

As you've probably already grasped by now, I'm a big advocate of being organized. If you're organized in your home and your life activities, you can be *more* organized and *more* productive in everything else that you do. I think that basic task organization can help with every other aspect of your life. All the things that seem like they don't matter—doing the laundry, making your bed, opening your mail—are more important than they seem on the surface.

So let's talk about making the bed. There's a military philosophy behind what I'm advocating. If you pop out of bed every day and make your bed immediately, then you've already started the day with a success. It's a small success, but a success nevertheless. You've completed your first task of the day. You've been organized from the start, and that helps you to move forward through your day with that same organization. You can build on that success.

I practice what I preach. Every single day when I get up, I make my bed immediately, before I do anything else, such as shower, eat breakfast, or brush my teeth. Think about it. If you don't make your bed right away, the option of getting back *into* bed remains, at least, theoretically open. And the truth is that getting back into your bed will *always* look like a better alternative than anything else on your agenda. But this way, I take my shower, and when I come back to my bedroom, it's neat, it's tidy, the bed is made, and I have a mindset that keeps me going forward. It sounds like such a small thing, but it makes a tremendous difference. It's a philosophy that moves people in the right direction, both literally and figuratively.

Most kids living in a dorm room or in an apartment—kids who are away from home for the first time—are extremely unlikely to automatically make their beds when they first get up. Mornings are just too challenging for them to handle. As it is, they've probably been up late the night before, they're probably in a hurry to get to class, and they probably don't see the point of tidiness. But there are few things less appetizing than an unmade bed (and even worse when it progresses to having with a slice of stale pizza in it), as any kid who wishes to invite someone to their room quickly learns. The last thing you want to do is disgust your date.

I want my boys to go off to college at the very least *knowing* how to make their beds. I don't delude myself that they'll do it all the time (have you ever seen a teenager voluntarily make their bed, ever?), but the skill will be there.

And there *is* a skill to making a bed. I don't think it's necessary to make hospital corners, but I also don't think it's necessary to give up altogether and never even try to do anything at all. There's nothing that makes a room look messier than an unmade bed, and nothing that makes it look neater than one that is even moderately well made. It's such a small step, something that can be done so quickly, that it's silly not to at least try. If you can get your kids into the habit of making the bed at home, then the probability of them taking that mindset with them when they leave increases.

KID, MEET WASHING MACHINE

I taught my kids early on to do their laundry. Here again, I'm not just talking about the mechanics of washing, drying, and folding clothes. Just as was true for getting the bed made, there's a certain philosophy behind doing laundry that is just as important for kids to learn as the mechanics of actually doing it.

The truth is that once they're on their own, and Mom or Dad isn't washing their clothes anymore, the outcome is simple: Their clothes don't get washed. You know what I'm saying is true, don't you? And like it or not, when kids wear dirty clothes—or noticeably wear the same shirt for five days in a row—people are going to make judgments about them. That's human nature. Most of us expect a certain level of cleanliness and hygiene in ourselves and in others, and when someone deviates from that standard, we're going to make assumptions about them.

We're going to assume that the lack of preparedness (not to mention respect) people show by not valuing wearing clean clothes extends to other areas of their lives as well. Kids can see this reaction in others, and this can easily lead to issues of low self-esteem. So teaching them to not just pick their day's wardrobe from whatever's on the top of the pile of clothes in the corner (and you *know* there's going to be a pile of clothes in the corner) is a good place to start.

If left to his own devices, my son will typically wear the same sweatshirt five days in a row. "Mom," he says patiently, "it's a sweatshirt. I'm wearing it *over* a shirt, so it's totally fine." Well, maybe. But I keep pointing out that when you wear something recognizable for several days in a row, people notice regardless of whether that item of clothing is on the top or the bottom, and they make judgments about you as a person. We have this argument all the time. I'm not winning the argument, but at least it's in his head that we're having it.

And then there's the classic panic-stricken cry, "Mom, where's my blue sweatshirt? I need to wear it *today*!" When that happens at my house, I point out that said sweatshirt is in the laundry, and that if he wants to wear it, he can wash it. I don't want to shield him from the consequences of his actions (or lack of action). If he doesn't wash the sweatshirt, he doesn't get to wear it. Pretty simple, right? Conversely, if he wants to wear it, then he needs to make sure it's clean.

Now, let's be honest. This doesn't happen all the time. I do their laundry plenty, because they're so busy and just doing their best. But I guarantee you that they know *how* to do it, and sometimes get the "go wash it yourself" response.

My own experience in high school was quite the opposite. I don't know if it's because I was a girl, or because it was a different time, but my best friend Jane and I were both completely obsessive about our clothing. We used to keep notebooks in which we'd each write down what we wore every single day so that we wouldn't have any of what we referred to as "repeats." We even scheduled the amount of time that had to elapse before we were allowed to wear the clothing item again. It might have been a week, or perhaps even ten days. After that, it was permissible to wear that piece of clothing (we called it "recirculating") again. We sometimes had to borrow each other's clothes so we wouldn't have the dreaded repeats.

Of course, we were female. I don't mean to be sexist here, but it's a reality. In general, girls are more fastidious about things like appearance and cleanliness than boys are. And girls notice what they're wearing and what others are wearing more often than boys do. So there's even more of a learning curve if you have boys, as I do, because none of this comes naturally to them.

But it's still an essential concept. If you respect yourself, then you put clean clothes on your body. Clothes that don't smell bad or are wrinkled or come from the bottom (or even the top) of the laundry pile. Imagine your kid going on a job interview, or even just walking into a classroom. How do you think they'll present themselves? Is the image you're getting consistent with the best way for them to make a positive impression? Wearing clean clothes means showing respect, both for themselves and for others. What I say to Henry and George is, "Show up, and show somebody that you care."

Our kids are supposed to be learning how to be adults, but as adults we don't always set the best sartorial examples. And yet there are consequences for us, too, depending on the decisions that we make around what to wear. I've found that if I wear my yoga pants all day, it affects everything: my posture, my expectations of myself, the work I'm able to accomplish. If I'm wearing my yoga pants all day, I definitely have a more causal attitude toward everything. I sometimes go into the office dressed like that. When that happens, the way that I do things ends up reflecting what I'm wearing. On the other hand, if I'm wearing a skirt and a blouse and am all dressed up, it gives me a different stride and a different way of approaching tasks and activities. I think that you dress for the way you plan to do things, so what you wear needs to be a deliberate, conscious decision.

And kids need to know that. How they dress is a choice. When you make the choice to stay in your pajamas all day, you're also making the choice of what you're probably going to do for the day. But if you make the choice to take a shower and put on a nice outfit and go out into the world, I guarantee you're probably going to get something done, because that's the message you're sending to the world—and to yourself.

This concept isn't just anecdotal. There are a lot of studies available that describe how what you're wearing affects how you perform. There's a lot to the expression "dress for success." No one is expecting a college kid to wear a suit to school, but I think that if your kids keep the concept of "dressing for success" in their minds, it will serve them well as they navigate through life.

And then there are the bed linens.

Even if you can persuade your kid to make their bed every day, the notion of changing the sheets once a week seems foreign to most young people. So make sure that your child is equipped with two sets of linens for their bed. They take one set off the bed, they put it in the laundry, and they put the second set on the bed. Presto! A bed that actually seems inviting.

I want to debunk what I think of as the "myth of the flat sheet" because more kids would probably make their beds—not to mention the probability that more adults might as well—if we simply did away with the flat sheet. Flat sheets serve no purpose. They get pulled out, moved around, and often end up on the floor anyway. Not only that, but it takes twice as long to make a bed with a flat sheet. Away with them, I say. All you actually need is a duvet, a duvet cover, and a fitted sheet. It's quicker and easier to wash the fitted sheet, the duvet cover, and the pillowcase. And after that, making the bed is a snap.

Years ago, I watched a video in which Martha Stewart taught viewers how to fold a fitted sheet. It turned out to be easier than you'd imagine. I taught both my boys to do it that way, and I recommend it for your kids as well. They're more likely to fold the sheet if they know how. And while we're talking about folding, there are a lot of ways to fold towels, so make sure that you teach your kids at least one of them. Having a method that's ingrained in them before they leave home is essential so that they have something to remember—and use—when they're out on their own.

Why this whole section on washing clothes? Right now, you're probably thinking that your kids already know how to do laundry. But I want to challenge you to dig a little deeper. As with a lot of the material in this book, laundry is something we assume our kids know how to do because they've seen us do it hundreds of times, but that's not the case. They have to be taught. You have to say to them, "Here's how to measure out detergent. Here's how to work the settings on the machine. Here's how to pretreat a stain. Here's what to do with bleach." You've got to show them, or you can't expect them to know how to do it.

When I was in school—and I went to an art school, remember—there was always someone in the dorm who would put something red in the washer along with their whites, so all their laundry came out pink. Or someone else might do some tie-dye in the machine, and then for the next few loads, everyone would have colored stains on their clothing! Kids kept calling home, saying that their laundry was ruined. Apparently, no one taught them that you can't just dump everything you need washed into the machine all at once without any consequences.

ENVELOPES ARE MEANT TO BE OPENED

In the last chapter, I talked about the importance of your kids seeing you pay bills so that you're teaching them how to be responsible around managing money. But it's not just bills that kids ignore. If something comes in the mail and looks even remotely scary, the rule seems to be "Don't open it." Some kids don't even sift through their mail. They plop the stack on the desk and wait for it to magically go away.

My friend Robin's son is a great example. He was away from home for the first time, at college but living off-campus, and he was stressing out. He kept calling her because he couldn't figure out how to buy food or pay rent. He was constantly out of money, and it was scaring him. His parents finally came to school to visit him, and what they noticed when they got there was that all of his mail was stacked up in the kitchen in a pile. In that pile were the $500 checks they'd been sending him every month. The money he'd been stressing over had been there all the time.

Of course, at some point, Robin and her husband could have asked him about cashing their checks, but somehow, they never had that conversation. It never occurred to them that he simply wasn't opening his mail.

Here's the truth: I don't like opening my mail, either. Honestly, who really wants to open their bills? I love it when I open my mailbox and the only thing that's in there is my *In Style* magazine. But in general, of course, that's not the case. Good things generally don't come in the mail. We'd all prefer to ignore what we find when we open our mailboxes, but part of being a grownup is facing that the things we don't want to think about.

And what a great feeling it is when you finish going through all that mail! *Okay,* I think when I've opened my last envelope. *I'm safe. It's done. It's over. It's gone. I've dealt with it.* Just having dealt with it gives you an amazing feeling of lightness. And dealing with it as it comes in is the absolute best way to attain that feeling every day. It's a lot easier to open three envelopes on Monday than it is to open fourteen on Friday. Once the pile starts growing, it becomes harder and harder to attack, and it becomes easier and easier to feel buried.

This is another small success that can carry a kid through the rest of their day or evening or even week. When your kid builds up more successes than failures, the chances of their overall success becomes more realistic. Teach them to savor these small successes and feel good about them because, however small, success is something that builds on itself.

None of what I've been talking about in the preceding sections is easy to figure out, and none of it is obvious.

A study reported in *Psychology Today* found that procrastination has significant physical and mental health effects on college students. Sleep was affected, students experienced more colds and flus, and relationships deteriorated—all as a result of avoiding everyday tasks!

You have to learn it. Many of us learned it like Robin's son did: the hard way. If your kids are lucky, you'll teach them so that they don't have to go through all the anxiety.

Think about it. They're going to learn the lesson about opening mail one way or the other. They can learn it the hard way (by getting into debt, having a car repossessed, missing out on a scholarship deadline, smashing their credit options, and so on) or they can learn it the easy way, by having you teach them good habits around opening mail.

By now, you've probably noticed a common thread working its way through a lot of these practical activities around daily living that I've been advocating you teach your child, and it's this: Things that you don't want to know about don't go away. Ignoring something is not going to make it better, whether it's laundry or bills or anything else. Putting it in the background isn't going to help, and *that's* maybe the hardest lesson of all for everybody.

IT'S JUST STUFF

Why do organizational activities matter?

I can illustrate it best from my own life. As a realtor, I spend a lot of time walking into people's houses and looking around, thinking about how to best prepare the property so it can sell, and sell at a profit to the homeowner. I suspect that a lot of sellers think I'm completely crazy and obsessive once they discover the stringent standards I ask them to adhere to in preparing their house.

But in general, what I see when I first walk into a home is that its owners are holding on to—there's no other word for it—*stuff*. Their houses are full of things—stacks of papers, dusty picture frames, and clutter on every surface.

I do real estate rather differently than a lot of other real estate agents. I start well in advance, long before I'm ready to list the house—sometimes months, occasionally even years ahead—because I already know that the homeowners are going to have to make a lot of changes in order to make the sale successful. I go in, look at the house, and talk to the owners and tell them what we're going to need to do to get the house ready. There's sometimes resistance, but I've also had a lot of people say to me when we're done, "Our whole life is different. We don't live like that anymore." They undergo a major change in the way they look at what they own and what they *do* with the things they own.

On the other hand, some clients have been mad at me. I learned early on that people will sometimes get angry, so I tell clients in advance, "You're probably not going to like me during this process, and that's okay. You don't have to like me, but you're going to thank me later. I promise."

And then I take them though the process of getting organized step-by-step, because it's *not* obvious, and change is difficult. Some people will just work with me and then later go back to their old habits, but they'll also admit that getting organized felt good.

When working with my clients, I take them through their houses and always ask the same question about everything in every room, whether it's a Kleenex box, a pile of papers, or a plant that needs water: "Is it helping or hurting the sale of your home?"

If something isn't helping, I tell them they're better off getting rid of it, or at least putting it away in a desk or a cabinet. It's hard for some people to grasp the fact that not everything they own is a display item. You'd be surprised at what I've seen—a burned-down candle gathering dust on the mantle, four different containers of the same kind of lotion cluttering a sink. These things are hurting.

People don't understand how the accumulation of stuff can damage their chances of getting a good price on their house. But what happens is that a prospective buyer comes to look at it, and all they see is the clutter. Some people are able to get past it mentally and envision the house without the clutter, but many people aren't able to do that. And why should they have to make the effort? Clutter destroys clean lines; it removes any sense of peace one can have in the house.

Think about your own home, and walk through it mentally. If you were ever to sell it, would the objects you accumulate help or hurt the sale? My point is that all that "stuff" isn't just cluttering your environment. It's cluttering your mind, too. I don't know how anyone can think straight with so much stuff around them. And it seems the more you have, the more you accumulate. Until you have to question whether it's you owning the stuff, or the stuff owning you.

On the other hand, if you're able to sort through the things around you, that gives you the strength and confidence to sort through your life issues more easily. You understand what it means to cut through the clutter to get to clarity.

I know a lot of people who live in the midst of clutter and are perfectly happy with their situation. They'll say, "It doesn't matter. I know I'm a slob, but I know where everything is, and I can find anything." I would argue that a person who's capable of being successful as a slob would be even more successful if they were organized. Imagine what they could do if they didn't have all that stuff to sort through or think about every day.

Think about it. Your stuff isn't just taking up space in your home, it's taking up space in your inner life, too. In your mind and very possibly in your heart.

So let's bring this back to your kid who's getting ready to leave home. There's no question that it's emotionally complicated for them to sort through stuff with a view to change, but it's also a positive process for kids to go through. Making decisions about objects—what they'll take, what they'll leave, what they'll get rid of—enables a separation process to begin. One that's healthy for both kids and parents.

When I moved away from home, my parents gave me a Rubbermaid bin. All throughout my life, they'd been putting things in it: my baby blanket, a stuffed toy, my soapbox derby trophy, some high school memorabilia. Things like that. And then, when I moved away, they gave me the bin. "Here you go. It's yours now. You're an adult. Put it at your house."

It felt a little like a torch was being passed. It was a practical and symbolic gesture. It became important for me to have it and equally important for my parents to *not* have it. I think that going through a process like that with your child when they leave the house can be very helpful.

Henry and George each have a bin, and from time to time, I'll ask them, "Do you want me to put this in your bin?" If they win an award, do something memorable or significant, or even if they just write a brilliant paper, it goes into the bin. They each know exactly where these important things are. I also started a collection of ornaments for each of them that they'll be able to take with them and hang on their own Christmas trees.

And here's the knowledge that the three of us share: At any moment, either of the boys could pick up his bin and take it with him, and he'd be able to have everything meaningful right at his fingertips. Think about that for a moment. They're ready to go, to move on, and it's visually and physically apparent to all of us.

This isn't to say, of course, that it won't be difficult for me to hand over their bins and have them leave my house.

As long as the bins are still here, it's a physical reminder that the boys are, too. But in my view, it's healthy for any of us to rehearse our kids' going away—to live with the separation always in your mind, so you don't get clobbered with it all at once on moving day. It's both practical and therapeutic.

I'm sure that somewhere, my parents still have mementos of our childhoods. But those mementos are never in my face when I'm visiting. I think that my parents' practice is likely the exception when it comes to dealing with the past. At some people's houses, you almost feel like you're stepping back in time, with photos and awards and trinkets cluttering up every available surface of the living space. I'm not sure that's healthy. When I go to my parents' house, I love seeing what they have on display. What they surround themselves with are pictures and objects from the here and now, things that reflect what's actually going on in their lives.

Of course, once in a while, it's fun to look back at childhood pictures. But we're not children anymore. If that's where you have all your energy—if you're constantly looking at reminders of your past—it keeps you in a certain place.

CHAPTER SIX

WAIT—I HAVE TO TALK TO MY KID ABOUT *WHAT*?

I was recently having a conversation with my sister. She has a daughter who's a college freshman and a son who's a junior, and they both talk to her a lot, so she's become something of an expert on what incredibly stupid things kids are doing on campuses these days.

And there's plenty to tell, as anyone who reads or watches the news is aware.

Why are there so many dangers and disasters waiting for our kids? What makes these news stories—some of them tragic—so prevalent?

The real problem is that college-aged kids are still at a point in their maturity where they believe that nothing truly bad can happen to them. They think they're invincible, immortal, so they do dangerous things without ever thinking that there will be any negative—or fatal—consequences.

My sister tells me about these activities (and, of course, I had to look several of them up online because I'm too dorky to know what they are), and I find myself appalled.

There are drinking competitions in which kids ingest gallons of water; more than one college student has died doing this. There are contests to see who can drink the most alcohol, contests to see who can stay awake the longest, and contests to see who can have the most sex. A lot of kids are attracted to contests because they're feeling their way into the college culture, trying to prove themselves, or see where they stand with regard to the others in their circle. They start off thinking that the whole contest is fun, or funny, and then when it gets serious, they feel that they can't back down, and they end up in trouble...or dead.

Sex is involved in a lot of games and contests. There's the suffocation game based on kids' belief that sexual gratification will be enhanced if they're suffocating at the same time. Some of the kids who put the bags over their heads won't ever be able to take them off.

Remember the story I told about my nephew's roommate? He and his friend were just fooling around that night when they were speeding through those hills, trying to catch a little air. Then they slammed into another car, and that was it, game over.

When I was in college, I found myself at a party where an Australian guy was teasing me about drinking. "You're such a lightweight," he said. "You can't drink anything." Of course, I told him that I could. I weighed all of 120 pounds, and the guy probably weighed twice that. "Okay," he said. "Well, every drink I drink, you have to drink one, too." Yes, I really *was* that stupid. Five hours later, I was throwing up into the Hello Kitty wastebasket in my closet. I was sick for two days after that, but, of course, I was lucky. I could have ended up in the emergency room, or even dead.

Some kids seem to go looking for trouble. All you have to do is read about the appalling hazing rituals on college campuses—I won't go into the gory details here—to know what horrible things they can do to each other.

Every generation has its share of stupidity, and the next generation gets to base their stupid antics on the past. Your kids are going to ask, "Did you do that?" and you'll be tempted to lie and tell them that you were a model teenager because you think that if you don't, they'll take it as giving *them* permission to do something stupid. It's a fine line that you need to walk. It's okay to tell your kids that you did stupid things as long as you're clear about precisely how stupid they were.

That's the crux of the matter. The important thing is that you communicate the information that's essential for your child's safety. All sorts of kids, good kids, do stupid things, and that's why you have to talk to them about it. "Here's what could happen," is one way to start the conversation. "Here's what you should do if it does." And then you tell them whom to call, how to handle emergencies. You're not giving them permission to participate in dangerous activities, but you're giving them a solution to the problem those activities present.

These things are hard to talk about. It's hard to ask your kid, "Do you plan to go to a bar and drink while you're at college?" And of course, that's probably exactly what they're planning to do. It's an awkward conversation, but an important one, whether you're talking about alcohol or drugs or sex or any of the myriad potentially lethal activities that are out there.

The reality is that whatever the currently popular stupid activity happens to be, your kid will probably try it at some point. They're on their own for the first time in their lives, their brains are still forming, and the part of the brain that concerns judgment is one of the last to develop. So they're going to do *something* you don't want them to do, and it'll be tempting for you to say, "You're not going anywhere! Go to your room. You're sitting here until you're forty!"

You can't do that. But you also can't pretend that you don't know what's going on or what repercussions the activities your child is engaging in could have on their life. You need to be informed and to stay informed. We don't want to encourage magical thinking in our children, enabling their thinking that they if they ignore something, it will go away. We can't be guilty of this, either. Just because you close your eyes to something doesn't mean it's not there.

So how do you start these conversations?

The easiest way is with a story. Make it someone else's story to take the pressure off you and make the point less personal. This will enable your kid to hear the idea behind the story. Sadly, you won't have to look far for a story. They're everywhere—in the news, in your neighborhood. Unfortunately, it's true that there are dozens of these stories around, stories about cars smashed up in the small hours of the morning, about kids overdosing at parties, about a drinking game gone wrong. You name it, and you could pretty quickly hear a story about it.

In fact, you could just do a Google search and probably come up with ten stories in the first minute of reading. Then you can say, "Hey, I was reading this article...just humor me for a minute and listen. I know you probably wouldn't do this, but I just want to say something. I'm sure that this kid's parents doubted that he would ever do it, either. And I love you so much. I just don't want this to happen to you. Okay, you can go ahead and roll your eyes after you leave the room, but right now, just listen to me."

I always give my kids permission to make fun of me later, but I insist that they listen to me now.

IT'S NOT EXACTLY MARLBORO COUNTRY

The advent of vaporizer ("vape") pens has ushered in a whole new way for kids to be stupid. A vape pen is a type of e-cigarette that ranges in size from a standard pen to a large cigar. You use it to inhale heated propylene glycol or vegetable glycerin (the main ingredients in the e-liquid), and then you blow out the vapor. You can also use it to smoke pot or tobacco. The liquid you use in the vape pens comes in different flavors (the pens can actually taste like candy), and they're—amazingly—legal for kids to smoke.

Recently, I noticed that George was hanging out with some kids who were smoking vape pens, so I confronted him about it. He was honest with me right away and said yes, he was with this group of people smoking, and he didn't see it as a problem. "Mom, there's no nicotine in them," he said. I told him he was wrong, but of course, George being George, we had to have a long argument about it. Bet you know *that* feeling!

When I took George for his annual physical, I asked the doctor about vape pens. She was extremely clear about how unhealthy they are, saying that there is indeed nicotine in them. In fact, she was very forceful about warning George off them; she went on and on for a good five minutes. She left the room, and George turned to me and said calmly, "She's wrong."

I'd already done some online research, and George had been unmoved by the statistics I'd shared with him. Now, I pointed out that his doctor had the necessary degrees and experience to know what she was talking about, but George was again unmoved. I know when I'm not going to win an argument. But at least, he heard the words. They're there in his head. Somewhere. George is fifteen now and isn't listening to anyone who's saying something he doesn't want to hear. That will change, but it's a difficult phase to live through (for both of us!). That quality of having an extraordinary amount of conviction in his beliefs is something I admire and actually praise him for, but it can be frustrating. I have no idea where he gets it from!

"NO" MEANS NO

When parents think about their kids and sex—when they can *bring* themselves to think about their kids and sex—consent is probably not the first thing that occurs to them. But to my mind, it's the most important.

I'm pretty sure that I had no real understanding of consent when I went off to college. I knew the word "rape." I knew something about sex, and I thought I knew what rape was, but I didn't know much of anything else.

I know that it's easy for women to think that if they find themselves in a room with somebody and have sex with that person, even if they don't completely *want* to do it, if they don't actually *say* no, then it has to be okay. I think a lot of women think it's easier to just have sex than it would be to say no and explain themselves.

A lot of women of my generation endured what was, in fact, coerced sex because they didn't understand that it *was* coerced. In addition, they thought that if they spoke up, they wouldn't be believed, or they'd be blamed for putting themselves in that situation.

There's a lot more to the issue of consent than what we ever understood as kids.

The best gift that you can give your boy or girl is the knowledge and understanding that *they may only have sex when both partners want to participate in the act.* Sometimes, it seems that sex is perceived as casual, a "hookup" as some kids call it, and not anything to dwell on or think much about. You may have your own morality around sex that you want to teach your kid, and that's fine. But we can all agree that consent has to be the most important factor in the decision around whether or not to have intimate relations with someone.

Consent isn't just about sex, either. The proliferation of revenge porn sites makes it clear that people can be taken advantage of in many different ways—ways that can affect them forever. People have committed suicide because of images posted on these sites.

Beyond consent, still other things are important. Your kids need to know about the dangers of unprotected sex. They need to know how disease is transmitted. They need to know how to avoid unwanted pregnancies. They need to know some of the social problems presented by people's perceptions of their sexual activity. They need to know that sex with a stranger rarely has awesomely great consequences.

But again, for both genders, what it really comes down to is consent.

And consent entails communication. Having a conversation with a potential sexual partner is an essential prelude to the act. I've heard someone say that they would feel uncomfortable bringing up the issue of STDs with a potential partner, and all I could think was, *If you can't even have the conversation, then this isn't someone you should be having sex with.*

Of course, all of this is tricky for a parent to talk about. But what's trickier? Would you prefer to be welcoming an unplanned grandchild into the world, going into a courtroom to bail your son out of jail, or meeting your daughter at the hospital for her rape kit? Those conversations are a lot harder to have.

And it's not as if there were never any opportunities to talk about these issues. They come up in the news with alarming frequency, and you need to seize those moments to talk with your kids.

Once again, use the news as a point of departure for your own conversations with your kid. It's not like there's a dearth of material out there. You'll see these stories everywhere, even among people or groups that we normally respect. College athletes commit a disproportionate number of sexual assaults on campus, often in situations involving gang rape (rape involving two or more assailants). The news is filled with stories about sexual violence. These are all moments that you can use to talk about consent with your kid.

Of course, what I've been talking about includes kids who are being cruel, malicious, or mean. And that might not describe your kid. But to a lesser extent, your kid can easily get caught up in situations that they don't understand— situations that get out of control and go too far without your child even realizing what's happening. That's when they need to have your voice in their head. You need to have had the conversations so they know when to stop. Where to draw the line.

I'm not trying to enter into a discussion about the inherent goodness or evil in people. All I'm arguing is that knowledge is power, and the more power your kids start out with, the better their chances of not screwing up once they're out there. You've given your child boundaries their whole life, making them safe and watching over them. This is an excellent way for you to continue doing that.

THE HERPES GIRL

Along with consent comes discretion. As I mentioned before in passing, when I was in college, there was a young woman—a very nice person actually, which made me feel even more pity for her—that everyone called the Herpes Girl. To this day, that's the way I still think of her.

This young woman started dating as soon as she arrived at the school, and very soon thereafter, she contracted herpes. A diagnosis like that should be a private affair, but she talked about it. In fact, she told a lot of people. Maybe she was scared and was reaching out, or maybe she didn't realize how people would use her indiscretion against her, I don't know. What I do know is that everyone referred to her as the Herpes Girl thereafter. It didn't matter who she was or what she did, she was just the Herpes Girl.

If she'd had someone supportive to speak to, perhaps this wouldn't have happened. She needed to confide in someone but didn't know who to turn to. I'm not saying that she should have turned to her parents. After all, a sexually transmitted disease might have been too delicate a subject for her to broach with them. But there were counselors on staff at the college, and she could have gone to them. She probably didn't know that.

I learned from that situation. I want to make sure that even if my boys don't want to confide in *me*, they know how to identify who *is* the best person to help them. And that's the best advice that I can give to other parents. Your kid might not want to talk with you about STDs. Fine. But it's your job to make sure they know who it is that they *can* talk to.

Remember: Everything will follow them. Everything. The reputation of being the Herpes Girl has probably haunted that young woman for decades. And now there are even more opportunities, more options for getting a lasting bad reputation. At some point, someone at a party says, "Lift your shirt!" and someone does, and a flash goes off, and then next thing they know, that picture's on social media. Here's a lesson: If you take your shirt off in public, there will be a picture of it. I guarantee you. Somewhere.

There's part of me that looks at all this and says, *Hello? Didn't you get the memo? Don't take pictures of yourself and then send them around. How tricky is this concept? It's just not that difficult to understand the potential and wholly avoidable consequences of that action.*

The bottom line for kids is this: What you do follows you, and you can expect it to show up somewhere at some time. It's going to show up on Facebook, on TV, even at your job interview. It doesn't matter that you're only seventeen. The publicity will happen, and it will be held against you.

Not that you have to be seventeen to be stupid. We've got a lot of examples of people in positions of power and in the public eye who've had scandals around things that they shouldn't have done. Even adults don't think about how things will impact their work and personal lives sometimes. But indiscretions follow everyone. People have lost families and careers over photographs that were made public.

So how do kids learn those boundaries? Again, we seem to make the assumption that somehow, they learn them by osmosis. They don't. They learn them by being taught them. And you have to be their teacher.

In a way, all that I've been talking about is a matter of being organized and prepared. Talking with your kids about uncomfortable subjects will prepare them to tackle the real thing when it comes up, and having organized your thoughts ahead of time—how to approach the difficult topic, what to say, and how to say it—will make it easier to begin these conversations.

Sometimes, I hesitate to use the word "organized." Instead, I might say "structure." Sometimes, "organization" implies the term "control freak" (though I know I am a little like that), but I think it's important to have a *framework* for thinking about things.

A framework is a way of structuring information, of thinking it through. And in a sense, all of the things we've been talking about here are related. They're not separate. Keeping your house isn't separate from your schoolwork isn't separate from the way you think about interacting with people isn't separate from your mental health isn't separate from staying safe. It's all tied together.

CHAPTER SEVEN

SOLVING THE BIG PROBLEMS

Problem-solving isn't about winning or losing. Well, it's not *all* about winning or losing. What kids on the cusp of adulthood need is a framework for solving problems that will enable them to work through those problems constructively and in a way that's respectful of everyone involved.

THE CASE OF THE MISSING DIET COKE

As I may have mentioned, Henry isn't the world's quickest troubleshooter or problem solver. Let me share another story with you. Realtors spend a tremendous amount of time on the phone, so when I'm out driving somewhere with the kids, I'm frequently in the middle of a conversation with a client or another agent when we arrive at our destination. One day, I was out in the car with Henry. I pulled up to a convenience store and, as I was still on the phone, I said, "Hey, Henry, run in and buy a six-pack of Diet Coke."

(I should pause here to admit that I'm a Diet Coke junkie. I can't imagine getting through the day without my Diet Coke. My kids know that; my friends know that; everybody knows that.)

So in Henry went, and he came back with a six-pack of regular Coke. I stared at it and then I stared at him. "Henry, what is that?" I asked.

"I got you your Coke," he answered.

I just kept staring at him. "How long is it, exactly, that you've been my child? You know I don't drink regular Coke! Go back in and switch it."

This threw Henry into a total tailspin. "What do you mean, switch it?" he said. "I threw the receipt away! I can't just go switch it! Just keep it!"

He thought I was completely insane to consider making him go back into the store to resolve the problem. And meanwhile, I was thinking that *he* was completely insane. I couldn't understand why this sixteen-year old couldn't walk back into a convenience store and say, "Hey, whoops! Grabbed regular instead of diet."

So there we were, in a complete standoff in my car in the convenience store parking lot. Could I have taken the Coke from Henry, gone into the store and resolved the problem myself? Absolutely. *Would* I? Not a chance. This kid was sixteen. He had to learn that you don't solve problems by pretending they don't exist. (You might be sensing a common theme here with some of the last few chapters.) "Henry," I said, "grab that Coke and get back in there and resolve this issue, or don't come back out. You're not getting back in this car until you do it. This is absurd. Just go in and say, 'I just bought this Coke and I meant to get diet. I threw away the receipt. Can I switch it?' It's not that hard."

Henry was absolutely freaking out over it. And I was thinking, *This is insane. If you can't solve this problem, you have a lot of incredibly bad times ahead.* We literally sat there arguing head-to-head for five minutes. Then, of course, he ended up walking back into the convenience store and in fifteen seconds, he had the whole thing resolved and came back out.

"Seriously?" I asked. "Was it really that hard?"

"No, it was fine."

This is an example that what *we* think of as everyday, simple, mundane, problem-solving situations aren't necessarily that straightforward to kids. Henry thought, *Okay, you have to have the receipt. Can I even do that, return the Coke without the receipt?* It seemed to him that he was breaking a rule. He'd thrown the receipt away, so he had to keep the product. End of story. By doing something about the mistake, he was putting himself in what he perceived to be a confrontational situation.

This is one thing that problem-solving does: It shows us that what we perceive isn't always the way things work. Henry didn't need to confront the clerk, who was perfectly amenable to the swap. But the problem loomed large in his mind because he thought it was something that it wasn't.

I'll admit that the whole thing freaked me out a little as well. I was arguing with Henry, but at the same time, I was feeling scared. *You've got to be able to solve this,* I was thinking. *It's such a basic, obvious problem. If you can't do that, you can't walk out of your house and be safe throughout the day. It's crazy.*

Henry, on the other hand, thought I was the meanest, most horrible mom at that moment. "Why are you screaming at me?" he demanded. "Why are you making me do this?"

And I thought, *I am doing you the biggest favor in the world, Mister. How could you possibly not be able to figure this out?*

I don't think for a moment that Henry's a dummy. The truth is that most kids don't have the kind of consumer experience they need to understand that they can advocate for themselves, that they can solve trivial or mundane problems when they arise. They haven't had to call customer service representatives to straighten out a phone bill or return a defective product. Their parents always took care of those things.

One solution to the Great Diet Coke Conundrum might have been to keep the Coke and buy a new pack of Diet Coke. That was what Henry wanted me to do. But that wouldn't have been very constructive. We'd have spent more money and ended up with a six-pack of a soda nobody was going to drink. This is why teaching not just problem-solving skills, but *constructive* problem-solving skills, is essential.

LET PROBLEMS BE PROBLEMS

Problem-solving is a teachable skill, and I think it's one of the most important ones you can share with your kids. And it's also the hardest to teach, because as parents, our first impulse is to go ahead and solve problems ourselves. We don't want our kids to have to deal with difficult, negative, or potentially hurtful situations, so we step in. Besides, if we do it, it's easier. It will be done more quickly and efficiently. And most of us have a sense of how to resolve different problems because we've encountered them before.

So the first step in teaching problem-solving is to actually let our kids have problems. I wrote earlier about allowing kids to fail and experience the consequences of their decisions or actions now, while they're still in a safe environment. It's easy to want to take problems away from our kids, but one of the most rewarding things we can do for them is allow them the success of solving a problem and learning that they can do it.

Of course, they can experience this success once they're out on their own—they'll have to—but wouldn't it be nice if they could experience success earlier, within the safety of the house? If they try to solve problems with their parents around, then they have some backup. Parents can make suggestions. A successful conclusion is more likely.

It doesn't have to be a major problem that they're learning to solve. Recently our cable went out, and I said, "Hey, Henry, can you please go call the cable company?" You can imagine the response I got. "I'm not calling the cable company! Those people are crazy. I'm not talking to them. I may be talking to somebody in another country! I might not even be able to understand them!"

I was unmoved. "Okay," I said. "Be quiet for a second. First of all, I'm not here to do everything for you. This isn't my job. If you want to watch cable, you have to call the cable company. If you want me to, I'll sit here beside you this time, so that I can be available if you need help."

I could see Henry was flustered. "Just relax," I said. "Say you call them. What's the worst thing that can happen?" This is my favorite thing to say to the kids. "What is the worst thing that can happen here? Are you going to die?" If the answer is no, then everything's fine, truly. Nothing bad is going to happen to you while you're talking to the cable lady or guy.

So make your kids do things. Make them solve problems they need to solve. Stay with them so that they don't feel alone (and so that you can correct erroneous information they might give the IT person), but make them do it. *They* should make the call. *They* should troubleshoot. *They* should answer the front door and deal with the cookie salesperson. Let them do as much stuff as possible at all times.

Earlier in the book, I talked about allowing your kids to experience the consequences of their actions and behavior. That works in a positive way, too. Once they've made the call, once the cable is back on, they'll have such a sense of accomplishment. Don't let your kid leave your home without experiencing that.

And there's a bonus to all this! They'll have experienced problem solving and so will be better equipped when new and different problems present themselves. It may be a conflict at school, an issue with an adult, such as a teacher or a pastor, or the need to call a plumber. Whatever problem comes up, they'll have resources to draw on.

Hopefully, they'll come to you with a problem, and you can help by talking them through it. "What are your options?" you can ask them. "What are you thinking about doing?"

Here's a conversation I can imagine: Let's say your child is in trouble for missing a varsity sport practice. Your job is to confront it straight on. "Well, what are you going to do?" you ask.

Your kid is hoping that you'll solve the problem. "Call my coach for me?" they say.

"No," you say. "This is where you step up and start being a grown-up. You missed the practice; you need to deal with it. What will happen if you call the coach? They might be mad, but they'll appreciate you taking responsibility, too."

All you have to do is just walk through the problem with them. You don't have to leave them hanging, but take every possible opportunity to let *them* solve the problem.

If you make the problem go away for your kid, I can guarantee that the same problem will come up again. And again.

You can also teach your kids as you deal with your own problems and dilemmas. If something problematic comes up for me, I'll share it with the boys. I'll say, "Hey, this thing happened. Here's what I'm thinking about doing." I let them in on conflicts I'm having at work, or even sometimes minor personal conflicts. "Oh, I was thinking about going to this get-together," I tell them, "but then this other thing happened. What do you think?" And I listen to what they have to say. I actually listen hard to what their answer is. This gets them thinking, and since it's not their problem, there's no emotional baggage attached. They can be more clear-headed. And it all adds up to experience that they can use later.

BREAK IT UP

One thing that's important for kids to understand—and that makes problem-solving less frightening—is that you don't have to solve every problem in one fell swoop. Every problem can be broken down into smaller parts—into clear, concrete steps that can be taken to solve it.

That's where some of my beloved lists come in. Write down what the problem is and the actions that you can take to deal with each part of it. Instantly, the sense of impending doom lifts as kids see that this big menacing thing is, in fact, solvable.

Even the most dire of problems can be confronted and broken up into tasks to fix them. "Wait—you're failing four classes?" Okay, *there's* a reason to panic! It would be so easy to completely fall to pieces in this situation, but it's not impossible to solve it. All you have to do is step back and imagine a series of interventions: "Okay, the goal is to get your grades up. Can you list exactly what you need to do in each class to improve? How about if you come up with some specific study hours? Can you go into the study hall help session every day at lunch?"

Just break it down into pieces. Make a plan together. There's nothing that cannot be broken into smaller components, and smaller components are invariably easier to deal with.

Most of all, don't try to do it *for* your kid. Instead, do it *with* your kid. Just like parents, kids learn by doing.

Anytime you talk to someone who's feeling completely overwhelmed, you'll notice that they're talking about something that feels tremendous. And it often is something huge that cannot be solved with one sole intervention. The key to losing the sense of being overwhelmed is to break everything down, and then write it down. Once you write something down, you have some degree of control over it, and you can see where the components fall into place.

WINNING AND LOSING

Every problem has three possible solution outcomes or results: win-win, win-lose, lose-lose. That's it. The concept is pretty easy. Win-win is, obviously, where everybody is happy with the outcome, though it doesn't mean that everyone involved got exactly what they wanted. Everyone instead got *just enough* of what they wanted to make the solution work for them, so they're satisfied with the outcome. Win-lose is typically where somebody came out on top and there's somebody on the other side feeling pretty bad about the way things were resolved. A lose-lose is the worst. Everyone's mad. The resolution wasn't good for anyone.

I can give clear examples from my work. When I'm negotiating a transaction in real estate, a win-win is typically when both the buyer and the seller feel satisfied with the outcome of the negotiations. If a property has been on the market for more than one week, the seller probably isn't going to get full price for it, much less anything over their asking price. So once an interested party shows up, we get to work. The buyer's agent is negotiating for the buyer, and I'm representing the seller, and together, we're going to come to some kind of agreement that the seller can live with and the buyer can live with. Maybe the seller takes ten thousand dollars less on their asking price because the buyer is willing to close in thirty days versus sixty. That's an example of a win-win, where everybody is satisfied.

An example of a win-lose situation is when is an out-of-towner flies in from Atlanta or Charleston and has to buy something quickly because their new job starts in two weeks. The market I represent has very little inventory, and properties are selling fast, sometimes at well over the asking price. So the buyer arrives from someplace that's less expensive and finds that there are only four houses in their price range to pick from. Three of the houses don't meet the buyer's criteria, but they have to buy a house, which leaves the seller holding all the cards. The buyer is forced to pay way over the asking price because they have no other choice and need a home. The seller is thrilled, but the buyer feels like they lost in the negotiation because they were forced to pay a high price.

Let's say that during the inspection, the buyer discovers a defect in the house, but the seller is unwilling to fix it. "Either buy the house or don't buy the house," says the seller. "We don't care, because we've got three other parties waiting to buy it if you don't." Big win for the seller, another loss for the buyer. The buyer loses because there is no choice—no way to solve the problem other than by doing what they don't want to do. Another win-lose.

Lastly, the final possible outcome, lose-lose, could be illustrated by two people going into a negotiation that escalates into an argument. "We're not doing that," says the buyer. "Well, *we're* not doing *that*," says the seller. The argument keeps going back and forth until the buyer just says, "Well, forget it," and goes away, and the seller says, "Fine." The seller doesn't sell their house, and the buyer doesn't have a house, so nobody gets what they want. They just shoot themselves in the foot. Neither one accomplishes their goal. It ends up being a loss for everyone.

In the two relatively positive scenarios, successful negotiation often involves compromise, and that's a difficult concept for kids to work with. Let's face it, there isn't a lot of compromising happening at home. You set boundaries for your kids, and they either respect them or they don't. It's pretty much cut-and-dried. And while they may not always see it this way, you know that by and large, your kids' lives have been outstandingly good at home.

That's because you care about them, and you've tried to give them the best life you could. You've sacrificed for them. You've lost sleep because of them. You've given up things that you wanted so you could give them things they wanted. And then they go out into the world and find that the world cares about them *just* a tiny bit less than their parents did!

So your kid heads off to college. A win-win for them will be that they do their work, hand in their paper on time, and get good grades. Your kid is happy. You're happy. Their professors are happy. It's a win-win. Everybody's doing great.

But let's say that your kid is struggling and doesn't want anyone to know. Maybe they're having too good a time being away from home. Maybe they're not focusing on the material. Whatever the reason, they haven't done enough preparation, and suddenly they find themselves up for forty-eight hours straight writing the paper that they should have started a month earlier. They finish it, hand it in and get a good grade on it. The professor is happy, and so is your kid (about *this* paper, anyway). So this is a win. But your kid is exhausted and struggling, and they still have other work to hand in and no energy to do it. Something will get dropped or will be subpar, and so this is a loss. A subtle one, perhaps, but a loss all the same.

And then there's the final scenario, in which a professor has taken a dislike to your kid and keeps after them. "I'm not happy with your work," the professor tells them. "You never pay attention. I'm going to kick you out of my class or give you an F if you don't show up." Your kid tells you, "My professor is a real jerk. He's always riding me and never picks on anyone else. I just can't win." One possible solution is for your kid to give up. "Fine. I don't care," your kid might say. "I can do whatever I want." Predictably, your kid gets the promised F and has to deal with the fallout from that. But the professor has failed as well. The grade point average for the class goes down, and the instructor's credibility is affected. In this situation, everybody loses. Nobody is happy. Lose-lose.

If we back out of these examples and just think about problem-solving in general, we see there's a moment in every conflict where your kid can stop and ask, "What would comprise a win-win in this situation? What can I give up that will make the other person think that they're winning while I still get what I need?"

One way to do this is to make the other person feel like they're part of the solution, and that's where compromising comes in. If somebody doesn't feel like they're part of the solution, they feel like they've lost, so your kid has to be willing to give in order to get. Any scenario in which nobody is willing to give a little is going to end up a lose-lose.

HOW CAN I TEACH MY KID TO STRIVE FOR THE WIN-WIN?

These real-life scenarios don't have to be hypothetical. There are examples of them in every family's life.

Here's a scenario that plays out with some regularity at my house: family movie night. I want us to do something together on the weekend, and we can all agree to watch a movie. But that's where it breaks down.

In the lose-lose situation, everyone wants to watch a different movie. I want *The Holiday*, Henry wants *The Pioneers of Climbing,* and George wants *The Hangover.* We argue about it until we end up not watching anything. And as a bonus, we feel bad about each other.

In a win-lose outcome, I pull parental rank and make them watch *The Holiday.* I'm happy, but they hate the movie and make it clear that they would rather be somewhere else. Anywhere else.

In a win-win outcome, we all decide together to accept a different alternative. We watch *Parks & Recreation* reruns instead of any of our first choices. Everyone has compromised, but we want to do something together more than we each want to have our own choice of shows. Winning doesn't always mean getting your own way, and that's a tremendously valuable lesson for a kid to learn.

Sometimes people don't even *know* what they want. What you think is the win is not always the win. Getting what you want can be a very shallow victory. Opening yourself to somebody else's point of view to make a compromise can be extremely enlightening, and you're often going to gain something that you never thought you wanted.

This brings us around to the major complaint that every kid has at some point expressed once they're out in the world: "It's not fair!" And they're right. Life isn't fair. But it can be a lot fairer if you contribute by compromising.

Things don't always make sense. And sometimes, you just have to acknowledge this and move forward. As the saying goes, it is what it is. In any situation, getting on the other side of the fence and looking at the other person's point of view is invaluable. If you always think that you're right and never try to see matters from any other point of view, you're never going to grow past where you are.

DO YOU FEEL ME?

All of this feeds into the concept of empathy. Most people think that empathy is a feeling, but in fact, it's actually a skill. And the first step in teaching and learning that skill is pointing out opportunities for your kids to put themselves in another person's place. The more they practice this skill, the more natural it will be to use it when they're dealing with all kinds of random problems.

The more you can step away from what you always think is right and consider somebody else's point of view, the faster you'll be able to solve problems. Not only that, but as I said before, it's going to open you up to many different ideas, and you're going to get excited about this contact with ideas you've never been exposed to. Sometimes you may even say, "Huh, I still don't think that's right, but let's explore it."

"Let's explore it." That's a good thought to have; I think about it a lot. Pretty much all the time, actually, double-checking myself. "Is it possible that I'm wrong in this situation?" Like I said, if you always think you're right, you're not going anywhere. There's no reason to discuss anything with anyone ever. The thing is, and I promise you this, you're not always right. Nobody is. There would be so many fewer problems in the world if we just looked at the person next to us and wondered, *What are they thinking about?* Or even if we flat-out asked them, "What are you thinking?" Because most of the time, it's the lack of communication about what other people are trying to accomplish or what other people are thinking that causes problems.

Another quick real-estate example is this: Often, I'll get a contract that has something in it that's making somebody on the other side very upset. When this happens, I don't just look at the words on the page, because these can be misleading, just as the words in a text or an email can be misinterpreted. I call the person up, or I go and meet with them, and say, "Tell me what you're trying to accomplish here. Tell me what you meant. Where are we trying to go with this?" Because then, based on that, I can say,

"Okay, now I understand. Here's what the seller is trying to accomplish, and now that I know what you're trying to accomplish, I think we can approach this negotiation in a different way." Just putting those pieces together, having empathy, and trying to figure out what the other person cares about puts me in the position to solve the problem.

CHAPTER EIGHT

BETTER THAN OKAY

—

The real question that every parent is asking is simple: "Is it going to be okay? Is my kid going to be okay? Am *I* going to be okay?"

And the answer—I'm sure of it—is this: It's not just going to be okay; it's going to be a lot *better* than okay!

That's what I was worrying about when I was awake at four in the morning, thinking about Henry. My fears for his safety were, in reality, me asking, "Is he going to be okay? Am I going to be okay?" When I made myself think about it, I realized that I'm actually pretty confident that, by and large, I've done all the right things for him. And part of that confidence is just putting some trust in my child that he listened to me and will make the right decisions most of the time.

Every parent has a time in their child's life that felt particularly special to them. I have friends who miss having a baby in their arms. I have other friends who loved their children's first-bicycle-look-Ma-no-hands phase.

For me, I am loving watching my kids grow into adults. This is seriously the coolest time. They're developing into the people they're going to be when they go out into the world. They're starting to grab their own independence—whether I like it or not—and this shows me that it's going to be okay, because they're taking the reins and saying, "Hey, I've got this."

CHANGING RELATIONSHIPS

Writing this book has sparked so many thoughts for me. More and more, I'm wondering what my life is going to be like five years from now. I might move someplace warm. I might start my own business. I might do some serious art. I might learn something totally outrageously new. Just as there's a whole new world opening up for Henry and George, there's a whole new world opening up for me, too. I'll still be their mother, but I'm starting to think in terms of not *only* being their mother, but being someone else, too. It's going to be exciting discovering who that person is.

It's important that we all do something about our future selves now, in the present. Part of raising healthy kids—kids who are ready to go out into the world—is showing them that we are healthy parents who have our own lives, and that these don't stop when they walk out the door.

One of my oil pastels from a recent show

You want to think about this before your kids are gone. It doesn't mean you immediately have a new career or a new passion, or that you need to move now, but it's important for you to look at your life and ask yourself, "What is it going to look like? Do I need to have a career? Do I need to develop a new hobby? Do I want to travel more? What do I *want* it to look like?"

I'm thrilled to be able to do that, and I'm positive that if you let yourself, you'll be just as thrilled. It's the reason I'm writing this book. I've started visualizing my life in a different way, and one of the best things about it is that the kids are still a part of it now, as I'm visualizing that future me. They're watching me develop it, and then I'm going to take it out into the world and do amazing things with it. And those things will be imprinted with my boys' opinions and advice. It's a neat opportunity.

The flip side to this, of course, is the fear that once your kids are no longer with you, then somehow, that puts into question your persona as a parent. "I've been a mother for eighteen years," you might say. "And it's exciting they're going off, but it's going to feel different. How do I deal with that?"

The truth is, using the example above, that you're going to be a mother until the day you die, and in fact, you'll still be a mother in your children's minds and hearts long *after* you die, so you're never going to lose that. You're always going to be their parent. My dad was at my house yesterday, fixing my bathroom fan. I'm forty-seven years old and a perfectly independent, functioning person, and I don't need my dad to fix my fan. But he wanted to come help me, and in that small concrete way, to be a part of my life. And *I* want him to be part of my life, too. Our relationship is intact. It's a choice a family makes, this choice to be together, even if in a different way than when the family started out. I want my boys to come home for the holidays. I want them to get married and bring their wives and their children here for decades to come—wherever *here* happens to be by then.

Change doesn't mean losing things. It just means change. Nothing is being taken away from you. It's just a shift, a different way of being together. That's all it is. Your kids are always going to need your support. I would dare anyone to tell me that their child didn't call them at least three times within the first week or two of college. Your kids will still need you. But perhaps they'll start needing you for different things.

How do you know if you're succeeding? How do you know if you're doing a good job of helping your child move into this next phase?

The mere fact that they want to move into that phase and that they *are* moving into it means that you did all right. Kids who feel confident enough to leave home and to go to college and get excited about going out into the world to do something, those kids didn't just get that way on their own. They had some help. It's because *you* helped turn them into confident individuals who know how to take care of themselves and handle themselves that they have that eagerness and that confidence. *That's* how you know.

Also, remember that you won't know everything about your kids or what they're into. No matter how many books they read or how many things you tell them, they are going to make a lot of mistakes. You're going to get some phone calls and hear your child sobbing on the other end. You might even get a call from the police. Lots of things are going to happen, not all of them wonderful, and that's okay. It doesn't mean that you did anything wrong. The fact that your kid was able to hold their head up and leave your home anticipating their future means that you did something right.

And then there will be the really great days. The days when you're completely aware of your parenting success because you're seeing your kid building character, a character that's going to sustain them through most of life.

You're helping build that character right now, through your own actions every day. And your kids are taking the example you've set for them out there, into the world with them. Believe that, even when you're not necessarily seeing it in your home all the time. Sometimes, I lose patience with the way Henry and George behave at home, and I think how embarrassed I'd be if anyone knew what they did. Then the same day, I'll get a phone call from someone's parent, and they'll say, "Oh my gosh, we just love George. He's so great. He can be here any time he wants to. He's just the nicest kid."

Remember that you're not suddenly building your kid's character the month they leave for school. Their character has been building gradually, over time, through what they think and experience and learn. It's going to continue developing once they leave, of course, but you'll also continue to see bits and pieces of what they learned at home.

When I was living at home—at my parents' house—I can remember countless times I rolled my eyes at something they said or did, thinking, *Oh my gosh, I'm never going to be like them.* And I look at my parents now and I think, *Oh my gosh, I hope I'm like them.* I think I'm like them. I think I've ended up with the same values my parents instilled in me, the same values I'm trying to instill in my sons. Frankly, if my children end up with half the value set my parents have and gave to me, they will be enormously successful.

IT REALLY IS THAT SIMPLE

Sometimes, life can feel incredibly overwhelming. School. Extracurricular activities. Pressure to succeed. Constant busyness. Henry and George are constantly characterizing their lives that way.

I say, "You know what, life is actually really simple. It's not that complex. You just do the best that you can do. If you're doing your best, that's good enough."

And the rest of it is simple, too. *Try your hardest. Don't lie. Apologize even when it's not your fault.* Those are my cardinal commandments.

"Just tell the truth," I've told both boys. "Don't lie. Lying can never amount to anything good, not ever. Once you start lying to people, they'll never trust you again. But if people do trust you, that can take you very far."

The part about apologizing even when something isn't your fault may be the most difficult to follow. A lot of adults haven't mastered this skill. They're not able to apologize, no matter whether they're right or wrong. It goes back to the balancing act of creating a win-win situation. Sometimes, it just doesn't matter who was right. There's almost no argument that's worth losing a relationship over, nothing that justifies bringing turmoil into your life. Sometimes, you just have to look at somebody and say, "Why are we arguing? I'm sorry. Let's just start over." The person that I consider the biggest person, the strongest and smartest person, is the person who can say, "I'm sorry. Let's just rewind." You're not always going to get the right response from the other person, but it doesn't matter. You tried. You were honorable.

Don't worry if building your kid's character hasn't been your focus. Just remember that much of what they're learning, they're learning from watching you.

When I say this to most people, they react with alarm, remembering all the times they messed up in front of their kids. Those are the moments and events that stick in *our* minds, but they're only a small fraction of what your kid has seen you do, what they've heard you say. You've also done a whole lot of good things in front of them. People are almost never defined by a single mistake, or a single moment.

The reality is that a lot of that concern is in your head, not your kids'. They're not remembering all the bad things. They remember some of them, sure, and hopefully, when you made those mistakes you owned them by saying, "Whoops. Didn't mean to do that, guys. I'm sorry." They'll remember that, because that's where your character came out.

Your children think of you as a whole—what they've seen over the years and years you've spent together. Of course, they're going to give you a hard time about the moment you screwed up in front of them because they can, and because it's funny. Don't worry about that. They might not even be aware of everything that they've learned from watching you, but five or ten years from now, a light bulb will go off in their head, and they'll remember.

They'll remember the situation, the challenge, the problem that they watched you solve, and they'll realize what it was all about. It's going to resonate with them in a way that it could never resonate when they were seventeen or eighteen, because they just weren't ready for it then.

To me, it's almost like taking an antibiotic. It's extended release.

We all learn things when we're ready to learn them, and sometimes, we use knowledge we don't remember acquiring. This doesn't mean the knowledge wasn't there. It was always going to come out when it was needed.

HENRY AT THE GAS PUMP

Some time has passed since Henry had his breakdown at the gas pump and called me in a panic. We still don't know what school he's going to attend, or whether he's going to take a gap year. He's been offered a scholarship to Seton Hall. We're waiting and thinking and talking, but mostly what I see in him is that he's excited about the future. That's also changed. He's gone from being scared to being excited. That shows him maturing and growing. It's also him making the decisions now, which is a big shift from me trying to be in charge of everything he does.

Do I think he can approach a gas pump with confidence nowadays? I *do* think he can! Whenever the opportunity arises to do something new, I show him how to do it or make him do it with me. What I can teach him, I'll teach him while he's here. The rest of it, he'll fumble through, or he'll call for advice, and I'll give it. I'll still be his mom when he walks out the door, and he'll still have a dad and grandparents and a brother. That support system will still be there.

I'm sure Henry is going to do all kinds of dumb stuff. It's the way it's going to be. I might be on the other end of the phone saying, "*What* did you do?" and he's going to respond, "You never told me *that*!" I can't think of exactly what it's going to be, but I'm sure we'll be in tears, laughing or crying over it, one way or the other. Hopefully, it won't be the police on the other end of the phone. I don't think so with Henry. But I also know that whatever it is, it won't be dull.

Just knowing that he's ready to leave home is giving me the opportunity to consider what my life will look like after he's left. It's also giving me a chance to consider what will be in store for George during the next couple of years, since he has all the same issues and concerns coming down the pipeline. In two years, I'll go through this whole process over again with him. And then, beyond that, will be the question of whether either of the boys will be coming back home after graduation. After all, the job market isn't what it used to be when everyone assumed they'd have a job offer immediately after college. But that's probably a subject for another book...

COMING FULL CIRCLE

I'm going to end where I began, with thoughts about where my family and I are and what our life looks like now, so many months after those nights when I was having nightmares about Henry falling off a mountain.

Those nightmares? I don't have them anymore. Writing this book was cathartic. It's helped me keep things a little bit more in perspective and proportion, and I hope it helps my readers just as much. It has also helped me understand the time it takes for issues and problems to shake out in a family.

I think understanding that is going to help parents get through the steps from *here* to *there*.

The more I listen to Henry in general, and the more I listen to him telling me about what he wants to do, giving me more and more information about himself, the more I understand him. Now, I don't see him falling off of a mountain. I just see him climbing the mountain. Of course, it still makes my hands sweat. My hands will always sweat. I'm always going to be a little nervous, but I also have discovered (and he's grown into) a new trust in him.

Graduation—Henry ready to head on out

For Henry's birthday this year, I bought him an incredibly expensive rope and a whole bunch of gear that I hope is going to keep him attached to the mountain. And I trust that he's going to be able to do it. I'm excited for him because I see he's passionate about climbing. We've come to a completely different place with that. I think that this is symbolic of a lot of things that I see him getting ready to do. I hope that the gear I've given him is going to keep him attached to a great life, and that he'll use it to scale bigger and bigger heights.

I'm looking at things in a different way than I did nine months ago, when Henry and I were in such a different space. Just trusting the process, walking through it, and not wanting to get all the answers in one day were key to breaking through to where we are now.

I'm the kind of girl who likes to get all the answers in one day. I like my lists. I like my organization. I like to know what's happening next. But with kids, you can't know what's happening next. It just doesn't work that way. You're not going to know what's going on all the time, so now you have to do something new. You have to trust yourself, and you have to trust them.

What I'm mostly aware of is that I'm really excited. I can't wait to see what Henry does next. Then George will do something amazing that surprises me, and I'll probably be terrified again, because what he does will be different from what Henry did. At least I know that no matter what it's going to be, it's going to be okay. Whatever it is, I'm excited to watch it all unfold.

All I know is that, these days, I'm sleeping through the night: no more four o'clock terrors. And that's exactly what I wished for!

ABOUT THE AUTHOR

 **KATHLEEN DAVIS** is a writer, painter, and Realtor who is currently raising her two teenage sons, Henry and George, in Whitefish Bay, Wisconsin. She studied design at the Savannah College of Art and Design and earned her bachelor of fine arts from the University of Wisconsin-Milwaukee.

In her spare time, she has spent several years volunteering as a coach and mentoring middle and high school students. She is passionate about the importance of education and worked with the school district of Whitefish Bay to develop its anti-bullying program so that all kids could come to school and feel safe.